She said, *He* said

An Incredible Marriage that Life Could Not Destroy

Becky & Jeff Atkinson

MEDIA.COM

To the God of second chances

———◗◖◗◖◗◖◗———

She Said, He Said: An Incredible Marriage Life Could Not Destroy

Published by
Illumify Media Global
www.IllumifyMedia.com
"Let's bring your book to life!"

Paperback ISBN: 978-1-964251-69-1

Cover design by Debbie Lewis

Printed in the United States of America

Contents

PROLOGUE

B efore Jeff…
My life was very messy. I had been married three times.

My first marriage was in 1980 when I was twenty-two years old and fresh out of college. We dated two and a half years and didn't have a clue about marriage. All our friends were still single. We were babes.

After eighteen months things fell apart. I was working at an accounting firm, and my husband was attending medical school. Basically, one night he proclaimed that he and a classmate had hooked up and fallen in love. I was completely devastated. I hung around the city where we lived for a while, but when they stayed together for a year, I moved back to Dallas, Texas, where I grew up. I was a divorcée at age twenty-four.

I met husband number two a few months after resettling in Dallas. He was quite a bit older and very charming, or so I thought. It turned out he was a real cad. My friends and family saw right through him, but I was on the rebound. After dating only six months, we married in a small chapel with family and friends in attendance. It didn't take long for the cheating, lying, and stealing to begin. I was also drinking a lot (a habit I started when my first marriage ended), which didn't help matters. Lo and behold, eighteen months later, we self-destructed. The divorce was a tough one. Finally, when it was all over, I found myself twice divorced at age twenty-six, but ready to start my life anew.

After all, I was still young!

I had a few unhealthy relationships for the next couple of years. I continued drinking almost every day, yet somehow I was still able to keep a nine-to-five job. One evening, my current boyfriend called me a disgusting drunk, and I finally faced my drinking problem. Soon after, I started attending AA meetings. I met husband number three at those meetings, and we began dating after I was sober for a year. Six months later, I again found myself engaged. Soon after we got married, I became pregnant and then pregnant again. I had two adorable little boys eighteen months apart. It was like having twins.

Eventually, this marriage began to sour too, and we grew apart. Even with a year of marriage counseling we couldn't rekindle our feelings for each other. We divorced after five years of marriage. The divorce was amicable; both of us committed to doing what was best for our children.

I remained sober for seven years, but after the divorce I quit going to AA.

Soon after, I was drinking daily.

After about a year my ex-husband number three moved to The Woodlands, an area just north of Houston and around a three-hour drive from Dallas. The distance between us put a real damper on his visits with the kids. He pitched the family-friendly atmosphere and great schools of The Woodlands. Jake, our eldest son, was about to enter kindergarten. I was soon convinced. The kids and I moved to The Woodlands the summer of 1999.

Find a job... check! Get a nice place to live... check! Start AA again... check!

Then, I saw Jeff at the pool. That's when our story begins.

✛ ✛ ✛

Before Becky...

I also married at twenty-two, purchased my first house at twenty-five, and with no kids, I pretty much did whatever pleased me. Then came my thirties, and I began to shift my focus toward career goals and even thought about having a family. What didn't shift was the "me factor." I didn't want anyone, anything, or any place getting in the way of my career opportunities, and that conflicted with my wife's values and vision. It led to resentment on my part and eventually an affair of the heart. By the closing months of my thirty-sixth year, I was ready to move out and move on. We divorced after fourteen years of marriage. I claimed irreconcilable differences, and she claimed infidelity. Whether emotional or physical, it didn't matter in the eyes of God. The truth is I cheated on my wife.

I moved from Virginia to Colorado and reconnected with the engineering team I had been a part of in my early thirties. Thanks to a close friend, I also began attending church, but I wondered whether after twenty years of living for myself, did God really want me in church worshipping and singing praise songs?

My transformation into a Colorado mountain person happened quickly. All it took was seeing a fourteen-thousand-foot snow-capped peak backdropped by clear blue sky. The days of living and playing on the water were over, and I was good with it.

I fell in love not just with the mountains but with a beautiful, vibrant woman twelve years my junior who had the stamina to keep up with a guy who was not ready to relinquish the adventuresome boy inside him. We married at sunset in a mountain church, declaring our vows to each other as a golden retriever frolicked in a snow-covered meadow just beyond the church's sanctuary windows.

The honeymoon was barely over before my smiling bride beamed and announced, "I'm pregnant!" Eight months later our precious, healthy, preemie daughter Brook was born. Two and half years later Bryce, our son, was born. Life as a father changed me for the better in many ways, but what didn't change was my "career comes first" attitude.

Six years into our wonderful life in Colorado, I accepted a promotion that moved us out of the mountains and down to hazy, hot, and humid East Texas. A colleague from Colorado asked me what it was like to live in Houston. "You walk around in wet underwear from April through October, and everyone owns a pool out of self-defense against the brutal heat," I replied.

My red Jeep Wrangler didn't have air conditioning. You don't need it when you live in the Colorado mountains. All you need is a soft top to drop down and soak up the rays. Goes without saying that Jeep got traded in pronto.

The family loved Texas. They loved our neighborhood in The Woodlands, and Brook, who was just beginning elementary school, could walk a block down the street to school, where she spent the day with all her newfound friends. On Thanksgivings we deep-fried a turkey in the driveway with neighbors, and during Christmas I donned a Santa cap while wearing a sweatshirt, shorts, and sandals. We also found a real connection to a young but growing non-denominational church that worshipped in the local high school gym on Sundays.

Family life was good, but I never lost focus of my job, a job that didn't leave my mind, twenty-four seven. A job where every day I lived and died by the numbers produced. I loved my family and tried to find joy when we were together, but my work never truly left my thoughts when I was around them.

Paying attention to the details at work led to financial rewards and to corporate recognition for me. Ignoring my wife's needs, sacrificing time with her so I could devote more time to work, led to a failed marriage and kids whose father would no longer be coming home to them every night.

Close friends and that loving church in the high school gym helped me not lose my faith in God's power to mend a broken man. Christ also gave me the wisdom and power to heal from the guilt of failure. Without it I would never have been prepared to embrace the abundant life waiting for Becky and me… at the pool.

CHAPTER 1

FALLING IN LOVE

The warm sun feels good on my shoulders as my two sons and I (Becky) jog to the pool. It's a Saturday in early June 1999, and the kids and I are going to have some fun playing in the pool and sunbathing at our new apartment complex in The Woodlands, Texas, where we moved just a few weeks ago.

I'm a big fan of soaking up the sun, even though a lot of people frown upon it.

Walking toward us on the sidewalk is a cute guy with his arms full of laundry.

"Hi!" I say as we pass each other, and he smiles.

Wow! What a great smile. I'm thinking he must be divorced because who else uses the communal laundry facilities.

"You must be divorced," I say confidently.

He laughs and I am smitten.

✦ ✦ ✦

My two kids are with their mom this Saturday morning, and I (Jeff) have the day to myself. Since the end of my marriage exercise and tennis have been my stress releases, so it's time to hit the gym and work up a good sweat.

I've warmed up on the elliptical and am knocking out a few lunges when I see her setting up for a day at the pool with her two young boys. Her sons look to be about the same age as my daughter, Brook, and son, Bryce.

She's a beautiful blonde. I wonder if she is single, I think to myself. *Okay, Jeff, it's time!*

Geez, I'm nervous. My mind is racing. *Jeff, you haven't dated much less interacted with a woman since the separation and divorce.*

The courage starts to slowly build inside of me and the nerves begin to lessen. *It's time. Drop the weights and the excuses, just walk out to the pool,* I tell myself.

I approach cautiously, and her smile puts me at ease.

"Hi, I'm Jeff."

"Hi, I'm Becky."

Instantly, the blood drains from my face. My expression says it all: *Another Becky?* I quickly recover, the color returns to my face, and I find my voice again. I hear myself asking her if she knows any babysitters to recommend, explaining that I also have two small children who stay with me on Wednesday nights and every other weekend.

Great pickup line, I think sarcastically. But apparently it seems to be working for me.

✦ ✦ ✦

I have such a big crush on Jeff. When I'm around him I get chills up and down my spine; I feel all giddy and jazzed inside. I can't think of anything but him. I feel crazy but in a good way. I mostly see him at the apartment's pool on the weekends. As I sit with my other divorced girlfriends, sunbathing in the loungers by the pool, I'm watching Jeff interacting with his single tennis buddies and playing with the kids in the pool. He appears to be such a fun person to know.

Our four kids are having a great time playing together, jumping and splashing and climbing the rock waterfall. They are all just enjoying being kids.

✤ ✤ ✤

"Bryce, let's go for a walk. It's too nice an evening to stay inside," I exclaim.

So, we head out for a short walk on the path that weaves through our apartment complex, leaving Brook to finish her homework. It's a warm, late spring evening, almost summer like.

Becky is on my mind and has been since we first met at the pool. I can't get over how good those few moments with her have made me feel.

While Bryce and I are conversing about the latest *Power Ranger* episode, I see Becky and her white miniature poodle, Mickey, approaching. She appears happy to see me; I know I'm thrilled to see her. I introduce Bryce to Becky, and we exchange pleasantries before chatting for a few minutes while Bryce pets Mickey. We find ourselves saying goodbye and heading off in opposite directions sooner than I sense either of us really desires.

Bryce and I picked up where we left off on our Ranger talk. Then out of nowhere, Bryce asks, "Are you going to marry her?"

I know all too well that Bryce has a history of trying to "unsingle" his dad. Recently, Bryce, acting more as my wingman than my son, introduced me to his kindergarten teacher at a Donuts with Dad morning. He loudly proclaimed, "My dad isn't married either."

Why does my face always turn so red when I am feeling embarrassed, especially by my innocent little son? Out of the mouth of babes—and five-year-olds.

"It's a little too early to think about marriage, son," I say as we walk up the path toward our apartment with the sun starting to set.

✤ ✤ ✤

A few weeks later I have the apartment pool all to myself on a quiet weeknight. Waist deep in the still, calming water, I prop my arms on the pool's edge while drinking a beer from a six-pack I brought to ease the aching in my swollen wrist—the painful consequence of being sent flying head over spurs toward the hard, dusty Texas ground while learning to ride a horse who decided to stop at a full gallop.

What on earth made me think I wanted to be a cowboy? I wonder as I take another sip.

I look up and there's Becky. Any thought of pain just leaves me.

"Would you like a beer?" I ask as she approaches.

"No, thank you," she says as she sits on the edge of the pool facing me, and we begin to talk.

The words between us come easy; I feel so at peace. *I am getting closer to being myself again,* I think as the conversation stays light and fun.

Are these chance meetings? I can't say for sure, but they make me smile, and I want more of them. Better still, I want to ask her out—and so I do.

✤ ✤ ✤

I've just gotten home from walking Mickey, my cute little poodle, and I'm getting ready to eat dinner in front of the television. As I sit down to eat, I think back to earlier this evening when I saw Jeff chilling by the pool.

He's so easy to talk to. What did we talk about anyway? I just love his smile. I hope he asks me out.

My insides get all jittery just thinking about kissing him at the end of a date. *Yum.*

✤ ✤ ✤

The restaurant is trendy, the atmosphere is perfect, the conversation is light and funny, the food is delicious. It's our first date. I think to myself, *You did good, Jeff.*

We are well into our entrées when the next words out of my mouth make me wish they had just fallen into the napkin on my lap before they reached her ears.

"You have a great appetite."

I can't believe he just said that to me about my appetite. Doesn't he know you never talk about how a woman eats? I feel like such a piglet right now.

The penetrating stare from that gorgeous, petite, woman immediately convinces me this evening is about to head somewhere south of the Rio Grande.

If he wasn't so cute, I would never forgive him and ask him to take me home right now.

Thankfully, Becky's forgiving heart spares me from a one-and-done date night.

✤ ✤ ✤

Becky and I continue to date, enjoying every moment we can be together. There is no denying it, we are rapidly falling in love. The amount of couch time spent kissing after her kids go to bed reinforces our feelings for each other.

Our kids are spending time together, beyond just pool days, and they are becoming great friends. Jake appears to be connecting more with Bryce. Jack and Brook also get along well.

It's a summer full of birthday parties at Chuck E. Cheese, evening cookouts at the pool, kids' sleepovers, and frequent trips to Skeeters—their favorite burger and arcade joint. The weeks and the summer months are flying by.

✤ ✤ ✤

A couple of years ago, I went to AA and had seven years of sobriety. Then when I divorced O.T., my kids' dad, I decided to try drinking again to see if I could drink normally. Well, I couldn't and didn't.

I've been sober again for a year, and Jeff and I have been dating for three months.

"You can't be an alcoholic," Jeff says to me over dinner one evening. It's a response he continues to repeat whenever I share my past problems with alcohol.

Maybe he's right, I begin to think. *Maybe with him it will be different.*

I know now that this is typical alcoholic thinking, but I didn't know it then.

✛ ✛ ✛

The kids are back in school now, as it's already late August. I'm finally feeling whole again. I can't envision my life going forward without Becky as my partner, my wife.

My engineering-trained brain intercedes. I decide to meet with my pastor for an added perspective. Together, we affirm this is the right time, with the right person, for the right reasons. A couple days later, Becky and I are at my apartment, enjoying a little private time. I pause, take a deep breath, break out my best smile, and then confidently ask her to marry me in a squeaky, high-pitched voice.

Her face becomes flushed.

I blew it! I think. *Where did that silly voice come from, and why didn't I propose to her on a moonlit Caribbean beach?*

Becky's hazel eyes distract me from my anguish.

The answer from those small, perfect lips still resonates in my memories of that evening: "Yes," she said.

✛ ✛ ✛

It's our wedding day. The rooms of the bed-and-breakfast we've rented are all decorated for Christmas. There is a beautiful flower arrangement on the dining room table where all the food will be arranged.

I'm unusually quite the chatterbox and my hands are shaking as I put on my makeup and do my hair. Soon I will put on my lovely lace-covered dress. Brook, Brook's best friend, and her soon-to-be stepcousin dance around the room in their frilly dresses as I work to get the finishing touches just right.

Oh, gosh, here is my dad to walk me into the living room where the ceremony is taking place.

My heart is beating so fast, and I notice three adorable boys in their black pants and black turtlenecks standing next to the pastor. *These are going to be our boys, our new family.*

Soon everyone will be sharing toasts, good food, and drink, and I can't wait to throw my bouquet.

It's turning into a perfect night, one I will cherish always.

✢ ✢ ✢

I haven't slept for days, and tonight is our wedding. Between wrapping up coaching duties for three youth soccer teams, Y2K damage control and holiday production planning at work, packing up my apartment, plus renting a western tux, all in the last forty-eight hours, I'm left feeling numb.

Thank goodness I am marrying the perfect wedding planner who can do it all, I think. *Otherwise, I would be staying in a padded cell tonight rather than our honeymoon suite.*

The feeling of exhaustion evaporates once Becky walks into the room on the arm of her father. The photographer is busy taking photos of the wedding ceremony, but none are needed for me. This moment, and her beauty, will forever be captured in my memory.

✤ ✤ ✤

After all the ceremony obligations, we are finally in our honeymoon suite, and I hear Jeff ordering champagne to our hotel room. After what seemed like an hour, we hear a knock at our door. Jeff lets in a young man holding a champagne bottle.

"Congratulations!" the man says as he closes the door.

My heart sinks when I look closer at the bottle. The label reads "Martinelli's Sparkling Cider."

I know he's doing this for my sake, I think. *How disappointing, though. We talked about me trying to drink alcohol again. Jeff doesn't think I'm an alcoholic. Surely this special moment deserves something more celebratory.*

"You look disappointed," Jeff says. "Hey, let's get the real thing."

He calls back to the front desk and orders real champagne. We drink some that night, the rest the next morning, and continue drinking throughout the honeymoon.

Reflections on Our Story

BECKY

Even though we had both lived through multiple failed marriages, neither Jeff nor I had given up hope on a healthy, long-standing, faith-based relationship. We didn't dwell on the past but looked forward to what God would bring into our lives.

Jeff and I worked hard at not repeating our failures.

JEFF

Having been through two failed marriages, I felt like a total failure as a husband. The common denominator in both disasters was me. I knew I needed to change, and even better, I wanted to change.

But change what? And how? This time, with Becky, I decided I would live as best this imperfect human could according to what God said was important for a loving, lasting relationship.

After all, He is the Creator of all things good, including marriage.

Questions for Discussion

What are some aspects of your past relationships that you see as a failure and don't want to repeat?

_____

_____

_____

_____

What gives you hope for a future, successful romantic relationship?

_____

_____

_____

_____

Who is guiding your marriage?

_____

_____

_____

_____

CHAPTER 2

THE BLENDED AND MESSY YEARS

⬥⬥⬥

Our honeymoon is over too quickly for both of us. Regrettably, we are not able to take much time off in December.

My first order of married life is bribing my two tennis buds to help me maneuver the furniture I have in my apartment down six flights of stairs and then drive it over to the new town house Becky had moved into just before our wedding.

"Hey, this is more than a two-beer job, Jeff!" My tennis buds, Brent and Ron, harass me as we struggle to carry the hundred-pound oak console TV down each flight of stairs. At every landing, as we slowly descend, one or the other has another snarky quip about how hard it is.

"Yeah, definitely more than two beers," adds Ron, as we lift the long, heavy couch up into the rental truck.

Living on the third and highest floor seemed like a great idea when I had selected the apartment. It had a beautiful view of the clubhouse and the lit pool at night. There were no heavy-footed neighbors above us to worry about, and the long balcony was perfect for Bryce to launch his toy army paratroopers. All that was erased by the logistics of battling tight turns and narrow steps.

"Don't worry, I'll throw in a couple of thick rib eyes to go with those beers," I offer as we begin to unload everything at the townhouse.

Amazingly, all my furniture fits nicely with Becky's.

"Guys, I can't thank you enough. Becky and I look forward to having you over soon for brews and rib eyes."

Ron and Brent, still sweating on a cool December evening, wave goodbye as they head back to their bachelor pads for hot showers. I'm guessing the topic of conversation driving home centered around never moving off their third-floor bachelor pads.

✛ ✛ ✛

While we settle into life as newlyweds, we enjoy the occasional drink, as I (Becky) imagine "normal" people do. When we go out to dinner, we usually have a bottle of wine. We also enjoy a few drinks on the weekends. If friends come to visit or we go over to their homes, we have drinks over fun conversations.

✛ ✛ ✛

Blended family life is seamless, or so it seems to me.

The kids, however, find it a little challenging and confusing as they try to get accustomed to new parenting styles. Having my children's mother raise her voice in anger isn't a shock to them. But hearing their new stepmom get loud when she's angry is leading to shutdown moments where Brook and Bryce just want to shrink away, or have Dad come to their defense.

"Boys, I said take your showers and get ready for bed," Becky repeats once more to Bryce, Jake, and Jack.

There's no movement as the boys remain glued to their video game.

"Boys—showers!" Becky says again, her voice rising ever so slightly. Still no response.

"NOW!" Becky suddenly shouts in a commanding no-nonsense voice that makes me want to jump up off the couch and go take a shower myself.

Startled, Bryce appeals to Judge Jeffrey. "Dad, I was just waiting for Jake and Jack to take their showers," he said in a tone declaring he is innocent of all charges.

"Sorry, bud," I say. "Dad sides with Becky. Go take it now."

Dad sides with Becky becomes a common phrase in our new, blended household.

Jake and Jack are also used to their own father raising his voice too, but that's not my style. Instead, I resort to the "Vulcan Death Grip" on the base of their necks to get their attention. This is something Bryce is very familiar with but never his sister, Brook.

The Apple of my eye has Dad wrapped around her finger, and that's okay because "Apple"—the affectionate name I have adopted for Brook—could never do anything wrong in the eyes of "Tree"—the name Brook has decided is fitting for her dad.

My daughter doesn't tend to get in trouble like the boys, probably because she is too busy filling up her social calendar— one that rivals any Dallas debutante's.

"Dad, is it okay if Missy comes over this weekend?" Brook often asks with an innocent expression that says please don't say no.

"Sure thing, Apple," I say.

"Dad, can I stay with Mom this weekend, so I can go to Carla's birthday party sleepover?" she asks, even though she knows full well she has already said yes to Carla's invite.

"You betcha, Apple. Have fun."

"Jeff, can we have a family-only weekend? You know how hard it was to finally get the kids on the same weekend," Becky says to me in private later, after I've said yes to another of Brook overnight requests. "Jeff, I love Brook's friends, and I remember the fun of being a girl with a big social calendar, but we need some family time."

Becky sees that the favoritism toward my daughter versus the other kids is sending mixed messages. *She's right. I needed that gentle reminder of the importance of family time.* "Yeah, it's pretty skewed. Sorry, honey, and thank you for bringing it to my attention." I guess it takes one Dallas debutante to know another.

✢ ✢ ✢

I appreciate that Jeff never yells. When he's angry, he gets quiet and has an expressionless look on his face. I call it his stone face. He also gets a fire in his eyes we all call "the look."

I, on the other hand, have a bad temper. I make an angry face, and my voice gets very loud.

On our first Christmas together as a family, we give Brook a cockatiel bird. It is eight inches long and gray with a sleek yellow head. This bird is a messy eater and loves to disperse seeds all over the floor. We keep her in the living room for lack of space.

"Brook, please clean up after your bird. The cage is filthy. I've asked you every day for the last four days, and you have yet to do it," I yell in total frustration. I immediately feel shame for yelling.

I inherited this bad behavior from my father, but that doesn't excuse it. It really flares up any time I don't feel in control—which is a lot when the kids are involved. I hope my temper will mellow out with time.

✣ ✣ ✣

Becky and I are equally yoked in our faith, and we make it a priority to attend church regularly, especially on those weekends when our blended family is together. It is important to both of us that our kids experience more of God's unconditional love, as the church proclaims it, in hope that the world's conditional love has less of an influence over them.

I wish my faith had been as strong as it is now back when I was in the early stages of my divorce. Even when my friends and church were so comforting, much of my behavior back then was focused on trying not to look like the bad guy and less about trusting God to lead me through the unknown.

Relying on God, being more concerned with how He views me, and praising His name in all circumstances is slowly becoming my default. It helps me get through life's challenges and not let my mistakes alter who I am and bring me to the point of despair. This perspective has taught me not to let others' opinions of me determine my self-worth or dictate my response in stressful situations.

Even though Becky and I attempt to do our best to lift our children up, we know it hurts them deeply when they fail, or worse, are subjected to cruel, thoughtless words from their friends or peers. Knowing that God loves them, we pray that He will protect them and lessen the pain they will experience growing up. The church youth leaders are incredible at balancing the kids' high energy levels with teachings on the goodness of God.

Picking them up after service is always fun. They don't like to leave their friends. Pulling them away can be as challenging as prying them away from their video games. "Come on, guys, let's go to Skeeters," is the perfect pry bar. Burgers and games, without fail, work every time.

✤ ✤ ✤

I have decided to take a week of vacation to be my son's church camp counselor. All four of our kids are attending this week of camp. It turns out better than the brochure promised. There are daily Bible stories, long chats over questions only a child could dream up, plenty of camp grub, and lots of fun activities, including The Blob—the number one water toy of all time. If you are unfamiliar with a water blob, it is a giant air cushion that floats in the water. Someone sits on one end of the cushion nervously grasping his or her life vest, waiting for the unknown while staring out over the massive lake. Someone else leaps from high above onto the opposite end of the water blob. Physics takes over. The force of the person landing on the blob causes the other person to shoot high in the air until gravity sends them plunging into the lake again.

"I wanna do that again!" is the immediate response when each child emerges from the lake. It's mine too when I get launched.

✤ ✤ ✤

I love our church, but some things really irk me. One of these is picking up the kids from their Sunday school classrooms. Jeff's ex-wife has also started to attend our church.

As I walk down the hall of the kids' wing, I notice her standing in front of the classroom doors, visiting with the other moms. Feeling awkward and self-conscious, I duck into another room at the last moment and hide until she leaves. There is no other way to avoid her.

How silly of me to be afraid of this woman. After all, I am married to Jeff now.

Jake and Jack are upset with me for picking them up late, as they were the last ones in their classroom.

When I find out she's also going to be a girls' counselor at the summer camp, I am furious. She will be there with *my* family. She will be there with Jeff. I don't understand why he doesn't realize how awkward and wrong this feels to me.

How will I cope?

As usual, I throw myself into my work. And the occasional drink helps too.

✤ ✤ ✤

It's been a long workday at the office. As I wrap things up for the night and prepare to go home, I notice my boss and a few coworkers having drinks in the kitchen.

"Becky, come have a drink with us," I hear someone say.

"Of course," I answer. I make myself a strong gin and tonic and join in the conversation. It feels good to be included.

After two strong drinks, I'm feeling a little shaky as I get in my car to drive home. Driving down the highway I think, *I hope I don't get stopped by the cops.*

I rush through the door when I get home and make another gin and tonic before Jeff and the kids arrive. I relax as the deed is accomplished.

✤ ✤ ✤

We've been invited over to our friends' house for dinner and a swim. It's the weekend, so I'm having a few glasses of wine while getting ready for the evening. At their house, they offer us a drink. By the time we hit the pool after dinner, I am very drunk.

As we are enjoying the warm pool water, suddenly I blurt out, "Are we all over Jeff's ex-wife yet?"

Oops, that will for sure piss Jeff off, I think.

Jeff gives me "the look" and suddenly pulls me out of the pool.

"Go get dressed; we are leaving," he says to me.

I hurried to the bathroom to change. *Man, it's hard to get these shoes on,* I think as I stumble around the bathroom.

As we're in the car driving home, Jeff says, "Why did you embarrass me in front of our friends like that?"

"I dunno. It just came out of my mouth," I slur back at him.

"You must learn to control your drinking, Becky."

If only I could. I hung my head in shame, sobbing all the way home.

✤ ✤ ✤

Becky and I have been married only for a few months before I am certain that she has been drinking at work. The smell of alcohol is undeniably on her breath when she arrives home from her office.

Deep down I feel that, just like Adam didn't protect Eve from temptation in the garden, I failed to protect Becky on our honeymoon night. I am racked with guilt. I'm her partner for life, and I feel like I'm failing her in the worst possible way. I don't know how to get her to stop drinking.

My sister was an alcoholic, so I am very much aware of what alcohol addiction can do to someone and to their family. I remember screaming countless times at my sister, "If you really want to stop drinking and get better, you would. It's just a matter of willpower."

Tragically, alcohol addiction led my sister to a premature death at age fifty-four.

How do I confront Becky when she denies she has been drinking? I wonder over and over.

I can't constantly call her out when she seems to be functioning okay most of the time. Even if I did, it would likely lead to verbal fights, countless tears, and threats that I am not ready to back up.

Can I be honest with what I'm feeling?

The answer seems to be no, so I surrender and hope the drinking becomes more moderate.

✤ ✤ ✤

The periods of moderate drinking sure keep the conflicts to a minimum, I console myself several months later. I'm grateful at least for that. But there's a voice inside me saying, *Yeah, just keep telling yourself that, Jeff, and someday you might believe it.* My mind wonders back to the pattern of my sister's addiction and I think, *You know the excessive drinking is coming; it's just a matter of time.*

It's just two years into our marriage and day after day, month after month, Becky's uncontrollable drinking becomes more obvious. It starts to affect our relationship with friends.

Just the other night, her behavior after having a few glasses of wine with close friends leaves me seething. The slurred speech, her venomous comments, the pushback when I tell her to ease up on the wine—it's all so embarrassing.

Far too often, Becky is becoming someone I don't recognize.

✦ ✦ ✦

I am already home when Becky drives into the garage. She gets out of the car and I'm there to greet her with a kiss. *Damn it, I can smell alcohol on her breath.* That moment I lose any sense of control over my anger. "You are drinking at work again!" I shout. "You obviously don't want to get better! If you really care about our marriage, about our family, about yourself, you'll quit, and you'll do it now!" I turn around abruptly and storm back into the house.

"I only had a couple of mixed drinks at happy hour," she replies, slamming the door to the garage behind her as she enters the house.

"Well, your breath says it was more than a few," I shout.

She stomps back to our bedroom.

I'm more than pissed off, but still, I don't want to call her a liar. She's the woman I love.

Simmer down, I say to myself. *You know you can't help it, Jeff, it's your nature. You like to be in control and fix things.* That inner voice of reason begins to take over. *Keep shouting at her and this special person you promised to love and cherish will just think you are, once again, acting holier than thou.* I start to calm down, but something inside me desperately needs to take action.

That evening, I bag up every fifth of liquor, can of beer, and bottle of wine I can find in the house and take it all to the community dumpster.

Becky goes to bed early and gives me the silent treatment. It's obvious she is still hurt that I confronted her tonight. *It was bound to happen, maybe even needed to happen,* I tell myself. *Yet, why am I filled with guilt at the same time?* I wonder.

"Becky, I'm sorry I yelled at you when you arrived home." Silence.

"Please talk to me, Bec. I don't know what else I can do."

"You have no idea the pain I still deal with from my childhood," she replies and then I hear her begin to sob.

"Tell me. I want to understand."

"I always felt invisible in my family, like everyone had only their lives to live and mine didn't matter to them. I am so tired of those memories." She pounds her fist into my chest as she continues to cry uncontrollably.

"Pound on my chest, Becky, until it's out of you."

The blows get harder and harder with every deep resentment of her past exposed until she finally stops and falls asleep from exhaustion.

My sternum turned black and blue, and the bruising made it difficult to breathe for days, but that night I feel empathy for my wife in a way I never believed I was capable feeling for anyone. I sense there's a closeness we haven't experienced for months.

✤ ✤ ✤

In response to Jeff's pleading, I've been seeing a therapist for a few months now. But I don't think it's helping me curb my drinking.

My son Jake has a Saturday soccer game today, but I don't want to go. *Those games are so boring,* I think.

"I have things to do around the house and I can't go to Jake's game," I tell Jeff. As everyone is pouring into the SUV, I head to the refrigerator. *Just a few beers while I do some laundry.*

Before long, I've had at least four beers and am starting to feel depressed about being home alone while the rest of the family is having fun together. I find myself calling Jeff.

"I've been drinking beer since you left and feel horrible. I think I'm ready for a change."

"I'll be home as soon as I can," he says.

He drops the kids off at their dad's house on the way home. As soon as he walks in, he calls my therapist, who has given me her home phone number for emergencies.

"Dang it, she's not home," Jeff says. He calls her husband, who we also know. He gives Jeff the name of a hospital in Houston to which she often refers to her clients.

It's taking forever to get me admitted to the hospital. Finally, Jeff signs me up for a five-day stay for rehabilitation.

Gosh, I really don't want to be here over Thanksgiving. I bet the food is amazing, I think sarcastically.

I end up on the floor for the mentally ill, where they pump me full of Valium and antidepressants, turning me into a zombie. I share a room with someone I barely see, and my bed is like a prison cot.

✤ ✤ ✤

This is so embarrassing, I think, walking into the visiting room. Jeff is here with Jake and Jack on Thanksgiving morning. I still feel like a zombie just going through the motions. Surprisingly though, I am still able to enjoy talking and playing with the boys.

I love these guys so much. I've got to get my stuff together and start being a good mom. I hope they don't hate me.

We talk about what they want for Christmas until they leave me to go enjoy my "yummy" Thanksgiving meal in the hospital cafeteria. I feel dismal about the future as I am discharged three days later. My head is woozy from the prescription drugs.

I hope the outpatient program is better than rehab, I think. But hope fades as the other students turn the outpatient meetings into a joke during our break times. My assigned psychiatrist continues to prescribe the same drugs. I am a mess.

I don't think I can live like this for long.

✤ ✤ ✤

I can tell that the hospital stay was miserable for Becky, but she seems to be making every effort to "work the program," as the Alcoholics Anonymous Big Book lays out in the twelve-step sobriety program. She is staying sober "one day at a time," and that's all I can ask from Becky.

This weekend she's with friends in Dallas at a self-reflection seminar called "Colors." I hear Dr. Phil helped develop the program curriculum. I am anxious for Becky to get home and share her special weekend.

"How was Colors?" I ask as we relax on the couch.

"It was an amazing weekend, and I can't wait for you to experience it," she replies.

She proceeds to describe the weekend's every detail. "They broke us up into groups of about ten. We weren't allowed any stimulants, so the mornings were brutal without coffee. Each group has an assigned leader—someone who has been through Colors at least once. Over the first two days they broke us down with questions and accusations about our past. Then the next day they build us back up with a lot of singing and dancing. You must go," she says.

As she describes what happened, I hear the same Becky I fell in love with. I can't help but believe I have her back.

✢ ✢ ✢

Three-plus years into parent school nights, soccer games, precision drill competition, and karate classes, I decide to accept a transfer from Texas back to Colorado, where Brook and Bryce were born. The decision is made easier knowing that their mother has recently expressed to me a desire to move back to Colorado.

The good news is Bec and I have six months before the actual transfer, so we have time to plan and organize all the details of our move. Plus, the kids will not have to uproot before school ends in May.

The bad news is that O.T., Jake and Jack's dad, is anything but happy with the transfer. In many ways, I cannot blame him. I would feel the same if I was in his shoes.

Yet, miraculously, all the stars begin to align. Every parent finally agrees to relocate to Colorado. O.T. and I find places in the foothills outside of Denver that will allow the boys to walk between homes, and their new elementary school just a mile from our development.

But suddenly, at the eleventh hour and without any warning, the mother of my children changes her mind. Long-distance relationships with Brook and Bryce will now become a sad reality for all the family.

I am devastated. My emotions swing like a pendulum, consuming me day and night. *How can this be happening? We all agreed to this move. There's got to be a way to convince her to still come.* These thoughts replay over and over in my mind, and my anger builds.

Sadly, there is no changing her mind. The fixer in me can't fix this.

Reality begins to set in. It's not going to happen. No longer will all the kids enjoy their weekly time together, no longer will birthdays be celebrated together, no longer will worship be a family activity together on Sundays.

It is painful and confusing for all the kids. It's gut-wrenching for me. Becky does her best to cheer me up. I pray a lot, and every prayer is full of questions: *What did I do wrong? What more could I have done? Why me? Why us?*

So we adjust, and life moves on, as the saying goes.

We continue to make the best of holidays and vacations; plus, frequent phone conversations keep the lines of communication open. The regular trips I take to Texas just to see Brook and Bryce are special. The extra effort seems to help us stay grounded in each other's lives.

✢ ✢ ✢

I'm so excited about the move to Colorado.

Finally, I can make a fresh start, I think.

Jeff goes out early and finds us a home in a mountain setting that looks out over the suburbs of Denver. The scenery is beautiful: aspen trees, ponds, streams, and grass-filled valleys where the elk herds and deer graze daily.

Still, I'm not thrilled with the exact location or the house he chose. It's in the same neighborhood where Brook, Bryce, their mom, and Jeff had lived prior to moving to Texas. While I'm disappointed that Brook and Bryce are not moving too (the kids have all become such good friends), I won't miss Jeff's ex at all. Before she changed her mind, I was afraid that Colorado would become a repeat of Texas.

To make things worse, this summer weather in Genesse, Colorado, is miserable! Lots of rain, fog, and cold.

I am a sun-loving, warm weather girl from Dallas, I think. *I'm wearing my sweats in July, for goodness' sake. How can I survive this crummy weather?*

I am feeling depressed again. I've also started drinking, and each day it's a little more. I know I'm not much fun for Jeff and the kids to be around.

✣ ✣ ✣

Brook and Bryce are coming out for a summer visit, and I can't wait to reintroduce them to the place where they were born. Jake and Jack are getting excited too. Jake will now have someone who will go with him to our neighborhood pond and help catch the garter snakes hiding in the rocks. I can envision them also digging up dozens of huge crawfish buried in the mud, trying not get pinched by their snapping claws as they collect them in a Home Depot bucket.

Trips to the mountains with the kids in the Jeep with the top down are number one on my list. If the darn rain and fog will stay away. *I never saw this much summer precip in all the years I lived here before moving to Texas,* I think. *It's got to be a fluke. Doesn't really matter,* I tell myself. *We are going to have fun, especially when we introduce Brook and Bryce to Guido's.* The pizzeria's New York style pizzas are each big enough to feed their entire soccer teams. Perfect for the appetites these kids will have after hiking in the foothills. And if that's not enough, there's always Beau Jo's Pizza where they serve mountain pies, according to their menu. Based on the size of their crust, I totally agree. Where else can you order a pizza by the pound?

✣ ✣ ✣

Christmas vacation is memorable. We have all the kids together and twenty inches of fresh fallen snow. All the outdoor activities that come with it are making the basement a mess, and for a change, I don't care.

There's also a new member to our family: Tubby, a fluffy, pure white bichon. He's become a great companion to Becky when the boys are at their father's house and I am traveling for business. The kids love him too. Tubby becomes a critical player in the newest winter game, one only two imaginative boys could conjure up.

Bryce and Jake hang the dog over the upper deck railing and release him into the nearly two feet of soft, crystalline snow below. Tubby is nowhere to be seen at first. Then suddenly he bursts to the top, bounding up the outside stairs to the deck, wagging his tail as he begs to be dropped again and again.

✧ ✧ ✧

April Fool's Day 2005 is a Friday, and I'm away from home for work. It has been a long week of intense projects with tight deadlines. *I've earned a steak dinner and a cold beer,* I tell myself. After a great meal I decide to relax in the hotel courtyard next to the firepit and call Becky. A strange voice answers her phone. "Hello, this is Officer Smith."

"May I speak to my wife, please," I reply after a moment of hesitation.

"Your wife has been driving under the influence, and I'm arresting her."

"Ha ha, very funny," I respond. "I know it's April Fool's Day. Put Becky on the phone."

"This is not a joke," the officer says. "I'm arresting your wife and taking her to the Jefferson County jail for processing."

I'm in shock. I need to reach out to Becky's ex-husband for help. I'm a thousand miles away and in no position to bring Becky home. So embarrassed, I make the call. "O.T., it's Jeff." No time to chat, I get directly to the point. "Becky has been arrested for driving under the influence. She is in the county jail, and as far as I'm concerned, she can stay there all night," I angrily shout into the cell phone.

Fortunately, he is calmer and more realistic than I am. "No, Jeff, I can't do that. She is the mother of my children," he says. "I'm going to go get her. I'll take her to your house."

✢ ✢ ✢

The arrest for driving intoxicated, the humiliation of her ex-husband bringing her home from the county jail, and the danger of losing her job, sadly, are not enough to pull Becky away from her addiction. It still has immense power over her, and she continues to drink.

Becky's drunken behavior is starting to scare the boys. I hear it in their voices when I call home on a Monday night in late April, while supporting a project in Milwaukee. *I'm catching the first flight back to Denver in the morning*, I tell myself after another incoherent chat with Becky. *Something must happen, and it must happen now.* I repeat to myself as I pack to catch my 5:00 a.m. flight.

I call Becky as I drive home from the Denver airport early on Tuesday morning, April 26, 2005. She is drunk and doesn't know I am driving. We talk for the entire sixty minutes it takes me to

get home. When I get there Becky is slouched down in the cush-
ioned chair next to the fireplace. She is alone with Tubby. The
boys have somehow gotten themselves out the door and on the
school bus. She's in such a bad state, it's all I can do to stay calm
and not yell. "I have to get you to the hospital." Worry tightens
my voice to a whisper.

At the ER, the nurse says, "We need to get your wife on an
IV drip and run labs."

Later, the doctor tells me that Becky's blood-alcohol level is
dangerously high, and she is dehydrated. "Once we discharge
her, I recommend you take her immediately to an alcohol treatment center," he says.

I ask for the doctor's recommendations, and he provides the
names of two treatment facilities.

We drove home from the ER in complete silence.

Becky retreats to our bedroom. I know I need help, so I call
O.T. Both of us agree it is time for an intervention.

He heads over to our house. Our intervention is unrehearsed:
"Get help to stop drinking or you will lose the kids," says O.T.

"You have two choices," I add. "A thirty-day rehab in Parker,
Colorado, or a thirty-day rehab at a center in Estes Park on the
edge of Rocky Mountain National Park."

Becky chooses the Harmony Foundation in Estes Park,
Colorado.

✛ ✛ ✛

Begrudgingly, I am on the way to a thirty-day rehab facility
in Estes Park called Harmony. I feel so anxious, as I have no idea
what's in store for me.

Lying on the back seat of the car, I am surprised to hear Jeff say, "Would you like me to stop and get some alcohol for you? It might help you feel better."

That's bizarre, I think. *I'll be in detox at Harmony soon, so I might as well start now.*

"No!" I answer bluntly. "I'm divorcing you when I get out of Harmony."

"If that's what you want, so be it," he says in an uncharacteristically calm voice.

Jeff has no idea how mad at him I am right now.

✛ ✛ ✛

It was painful to say goodbye to Becky. I thought I would be angry or anxious on my ninety-minute drive back from Estes Park. Instead, I am inexplicably peaceful. I can't help but believe it's "the peace of God, which transcends all understanding" Paul speaks about in Philippians 4:7.

A few nights later, Becky and I speak briefly on the phone.

"I hate it here!" she complains. "My roommate is a twenty-five-year-old meth head. I have nothing in common with her. There is too much food offered all day long. I'm going to get fat."

I don't feel very encouraged. I can hear the resentment building as we talk—the same defiant attitude she had on the trip up to Harmony. Despite her bitterness, I do not doubt the wisdom of our going through with the intervention.

When we hang up, I reach out to a few close friends and family members to tell them what is happening. I ask for their prayers of healing for Becky, for the kids, and for our marriage.

I constantly pray these thirty days will become a significant moment that begins to change our marriage and relationship for the better.

✤ ✤ ✤

I feel a little anxious as I walk into my assigned psychiatrist's office. It's been about a week since I arrived at Harmony.

"I don't care; I don't want to stop drinking. I hate it here," I tell him. I'm still so angry at having to be in rehab.

I am so angry and closed-minded, I don't remember anything he said to me as I head back to my cabin.

Day by day, however, I begin to feel the fight draining out of me. The evening meetings with the counselor and the other women in my group are starting to soften my attitude. One morning, I wake up and feel like a new me.

I give up. Jesus, please help me. I'm a hopeless drunk, and I need to give up alcohol forever.

After this moment, I begin to look forward to the twelve-step meetings, especially the group meetings with the other girls and the counselor every evening before bed.

I gradually find myself forgiving Jeff for bringing me to Harmony; actually, I realize I should *thank* him. I'm within the final days of my stay and excited for Jeff to attend the weekend program for spouses and loved ones. I'm happy he will learn more about alcoholism. It's crucial he learns that the path to sobriety isn't just a matter of willpower.

✤ ✤ ✤

During one of our limited phone calls, Becky asks me to read a book about alcoholism called *Beyond the Influence,* by Katherine Ketcham. It lays out, in detail, the biological reasons why alcohol alters the chemistry of the body and brain. It logically explains that some people are helpless to control their drinking, while others can manage it properly. It's eye-opening. According to Ketcham, one must be alcohol-free for at least a couple weeks before one can think clearly enough to benefit from group meetings, one-on-one therapy, open discussions with family, and quiet reflection. This healing also includes asking a higher power (which for us is the God of Abraham and Moses) to give you what you need to resist, to cope, and to release both the psychological and physical grip of alcohol on your life.

I now understand why Becky must stay thirty days at Harmony if she is to have any chance to succeed. Most importantly, this revelation changes how I view her struggle and what I pray for each day and night. It gives me not just compassion, but also direction about what my support role will be after Becky returns home from her time in rehab.

✦ ✦ ✦

For Becky's final weekend at Harmony, I have been asked to join other spouses and family members for counseling sessions. I am not allowed to stay with Becky, and she doesn't attend any of the sessions except for this one. We are sitting in chairs facing each other and the counselor asks Becky to speak first.

"I am so sorry for the pain I have caused you and others. Please forgive me and support me as I work my steps to stay sober."

I quickly respond, "I still love you beyond measure. I have forgiven you and will support you." I pause before adding, "But if you ever drink again, our marriage is over."

I want so badly to take those words back, yet I can't forget how difficult this disease has been on all of us. I also know the odds of relapsing are not in Becky's favor if she doesn't work on the program. All morning and afternoon the therapists and counselors have made that point crystal clear to us.

At the commencement dinner, Becky and I are together. All the family members are asked individually to stand and share their thoughts on the weekend. It's my turn, and I have a thousand thoughts going through my mind as I begin to speak.

"First, I want to thank the Harmony staff," I begin.

I am overwhelmed with emotion but somehow find the words to share all the hope I am feeling for Becky as she fights daily to destroy this demon with the healing and renewing power only God can give her

Becky hugs me as I return to my seat. It's a hug only lovers can feel when they embrace.

We are one again.

✛ ✛ ✛

Once home, I must pay my dues for driving under the influence. I go to court, lose my driver's license for ninety days, attend classes, and perform random breathalyzers and urine tests—all reminders of that shameful traffic stop for driving too slowly and erratically on April Fool's Day.

A significant part of my path to a sober, healthy life begins with aftercare counseling.

My therapist, who I'll call Ben, is easy-going and puts me at ease. After several sessions, he recommends I see a psychiatrist who specializes in treating alcoholics and addicts. My session with her seems to last a long time. She is very warm and leaves me with a lot of hope. She diagnoses me as mildly bipolar and places me on a medication regimen that should stabilize me.

Ben is also teaching me to rewire my brain by paying attention to happy moments as I am experiencing them. It takes some effort, but I'm getting used to doing so. I now hope that one day, I will be happy without alcohol.

✣ ✣ ✣

In his book *Disappointment with God*, Philip Yancey writes that "lovers possess complete freedom yet choose to give it away and become dependent." I believe Becky will be heavily dependent on me after completing her time at Harmony. But my beliefs are challenged yet again as I soon discover that it depends not so much on me, but upon God and attending regular meetings with her counselor. Those will be the two critical things she needs the most as sobriety becomes a new way of life. So, for now I try my best to be encouraging and supportive, knowing our dependence upon each other will return with time.

✣ ✣ ✣

Year one is slow and challenging. My heart aches for Becky as doubts about ever having a "normal life" try to steal any moment of joy she is ever so slowly beginning to feel. There's also the shame she feels for allowing alcohol to once again have control over her life.

I need to be patient. How many times a day do I need to say it? As many as it takes, I tell myself daily. All I want is to begin reconnecting as husband and wife, as best friends, and to have our blended family full of joy under the same roof.

Slowly, I see Becky beginning to realize she doesn't have to be burdened with the shame of alcoholism, that God does not see her as just a weak creation in need of His strength, that her family still loves her without conditions, and that her husband loves and desires her.

"Fearfully and wonderfully made," that's how God sees Becky. Beautiful, wanted, and needed, that's how we, her family, see her.

✢ ✢ ✢

When do Jeff and I begin to heal? It's a slow, gradual process. We learn to be honest with each other, to share our thoughts and feelings, to go back to church, and to pray for our relationship—a lot! It takes time, but gradually we fall madly in love, again and again.

Today, it's totally awesome how much we say "I love you" to each other. We continue to work on our marriage by serving God and each other every day.

We're both retired now and spend lots of time together: having coffee, taking long walks, volunteering, spending time with family and our grandchildren. I honestly believe we would not have the strong relationship we do today had we not gone through these tough times. It was so worth it!

Reflections on Our Story

While it is easier to ignore your uncomfortable feelings about your spouse's behavior, it's not healthy to do so. It's better to talk openly with your spouse about your suspicions. Then together, you can figure out the source of these behaviors and the next step to resolving the issues.

—BECKY—

Today, I wonder if I would have sought help sooner if I had known how Jeff was feeling instead of both of us sweeping it under the rug.

—JEFF—

The years in Colorado without my son and daughter were challenging and painful. There was a brief time they lived in Colorado. When Brook and Bryce were in high school, their mother moved back to Colorado. Unfortunately, yet understandably, after a semester they missed their friends and the life they had known for nearly twelve years, so they moved back to Texas.

As my faith continues to grow, I can now see how the arms of Jesus embraced us and kept us together, though physically separated by a thousand miles. God heard my questions, God felt my pain, and God never left my side—or my children's.

BECKY

I didn't succeed at sobriety with my first stint in rehab in Texas. It wasn't the right place for me, and they pumped me full of Valium and tranquilizers. My first psychiatrist did the same. Jeff and I needed to talk about how I was adjusting after that first attempt, which wasn't well.

What I learned is that if at first you don't succeed at the change you are seeking, try another way. Keep trying and never give up! My thirty-day treatment at Harmony was what finally did the trick for me.

Get correct and sufficient information about your problems. As a spouse of someone struggling with alcoholism, don't assume you know it all. When Jeff read the book I suggested about the alcoholic brain, he began to understand that drinking wasn't all about self-control. I was finally able to concentrate on my recovery without worrying about what he was thinking.

JEFF

We seldom talk in-depth about that pivotal first year of sobriety. I'd like to believe it's because we continue to have victory over a powerful, debilitating disease.

My promise to Becky before she left Harmony was that I would never drink again. Maybe my act of support has made a difference. But it's the power of God working through Becky that is truly the biggest factor in restoring our love, respect, and desire for each other that fills our lives every day.

Al-Anon, the support organization for friends and family members of an alcoholic, teaches that when it comes to alcoholism, "You didn't cause it, you can't control it, and you can't cure it." That is all true but believe me when I say you sure as hell can enable it. I know I did.

We attended and served at churches regularly in both Texas and Colorado. We also belonged to a life group with close friends when we lived in The Woodlands. Yet all that time, until Becky entered Harmony, I never shared what we were struggling with or asked our church leaders, our friends, or our families to pray for intervention and healing.

My belief that the problem was Becky's lack of faith and willpower—along with my own humiliation at our situation—blinded me to seeing the need to ask for help that was available to fight addiction.

I do believe God guided Becky's choice to go to rehab at the Harmony Foundation. Most important, both of us surrendering it all—all of our denial, all of our self-determination, all of our lies, and all of my self-righteous judgment—to God is what brought sobriety back into our lives. This brought us to a place where God could do His best work.

Questions for Discussion

How are you managing the dynamics of family or blended family life? Is God playing a critical role? If yes, how?

_____

_____

_____

_____

Are you suspicious of any type of behavior in your relationship? Are there any addictions that need to be brought out into the light?

_____

_____

_____

_____

Is one or the other of you manipulating the other in some way? What about enabling harmful behavior?

_____

_____

_____

_____

What are the things you love about the other person? In what ways can your love for one another help you withstand the challenges you are facing?

_____

_____

_____

_____

How would your relationship improve if you brought God into the picture? What are some ways to do this?

_____

_____

_____

_____

Chapter 3

The "Odd" Times

My (Becky) oldest son's legal name is Odd, named after his paternal grandfather. We called him by his grandfather's nickname, Jake. We thought he would be embarrassed by the name Odd, even if it is Norwegian.

Of course, on the first day of every school year, his teachers would be perplexed at roll call. "Odd? Todd? Is this a typo?"

In high school, his soccer buddies began jokingly calling him Odd, and it stuck. No one makes fun of him; they all think it's cool. So, he's become Odd, except not to me. He will always be my sweet, wonderful, adorable Jake.

Jack is not athletic at all; in fact, he's super clumsy. Thank goodness, he is also durable and has a high tolerance for pain.

We often hear *boom, boom, boom, thud*, as he's hurrying down the stairs to his basement bedroom. After a short pause, we'll get a reassuring: "I'm okay!"

He's finally found his niche in voice and theater. In high school, he's president of the theater club and plays the lead in almost all the musicals and many of the plays.

Bryce, like Jake, loves soccer and they both play on their varsity high school teams. He is also raising a pig as a FFA project, but who knows how long this will last.

Brook plays varsity soccer too in high school, but her true love is running cross-country for the Bear Cat women's varsity team. She also loves being a part of a Young Life group and is up for any outdoor adventure.

Despite how proud I am of them all, I have to say I feel helpless raising teenagers.

When I was a teenager, my sisters had left home for college, so it was just me and my parents. I often felt forgotten and spent most of my time alone in my room. Sure, I had friends, but we didn't have a lot of family time together.

I work a full-time job, which puts a lot of stress on me. To cope, I dissociate a lot.

The boys are fighting downstairs, I don't hear them until one of them runs upstairs and yells, "Mom!"

Jake has a homework project due next week. I don't give it a thought or help him with it.

Jack got the lead in this semester's musical. I don't think to ask him about it until the week of the show.

I'm a mom on autopilot!

✢ ✢ ✢

The teenage years are often the silent years.

"How's school, Jack?" I (Jeff) might ask.

"Okay," is all I get.

"Why aren't you doing your homework, Jake?"

"Teacher's workshop." *Why do teenage boys seem to specialize in using as few words as possible?*

"Did you get the part you wanted in the play, Jack?"

"No, and I don't want to talk about it."

"Do you like any boys at school, Brook?"

"Dad! No, and I don't want to talk about it!"

Sigh.

Communication is awkward, with short bursts of fragmented sentences at best.

But then, when you least expect it, you truly get to be a parent. Our one-on-one hiking and biking afternoons through the mountains—especially when my kids come to visit from Texas—have a magical way of starting conversations where they ask for Dad's advice, and I'm happy to give it freely.

✢ ✢ ✢

Family vacations are full of the unexpected when you have three teenage boys (twelve, thirteen, and fourteen), as well as a fifteen-year-old girl.

Our first Airbnb experience takes place in the Riviera Maya, Mexico. We have a beautiful third-story resort condo with a balcony and splash pool, all overlooking a crocodile sanctuary. "Dad, this is amazing!" declares Bryce. "You are the coolest dad, ever!"

"Geez, if I'd known a crocodile sanctuary bestows the Coolest Dad honor, I would have done it years ago," I reply with a bit of pride.

It's a safe resort, so Becky and I decided to give the boys the freedom to explore on their own. Not one morning goes by that

Brook and I don't go to the fitness center to get our gym rat fix on.

The boys have other morning plans: gorging themselves on a Texas-size breakfast buffet. They pile their plates with every familiar item on the buffet table. Stacks of pancakes and waffles smothered in buttery syrup, massive strips of bacon barely hanging onto the edge of their plates, and sausage patties floating on top of the syrup. How can teenage boys consume such massive quantities of food and fresh squeezed orange juice yet look skinnier when they walk away from the table? Unbelievable!

After a day swimming with the kids in one of the biggest pools in the northern hemisphere and having a delicious dinner, we take advantage of a soft breeze and walk along the beach. The family time together has been wonderful. The whole week has been special, but finally it is time to fly back to Colorado.

I retrieved the itemized bill slid under the front door. Oddly, there's a sizable charge from the resort pharmacy.

Becky sees my puzzled look and says: "The boys have something to tell you."

Heads bowed, knees trembling, the boys confess that they charged prophylactics to our condo, then filled the condoms to the bursting point with water and bombarded the crocodiles from our balcony.

I look at them sternly, while trying not to explode in laughter.

"Okay," I say. "Your punishment is to have unprotected sex for the next month!"

That goes right over their heads, I guess, based upon the three blank stares I get in return.

✦ ✦ ✦

Yippee, another super fun family trip!

The kids are now ages fourteen to seventeen, and this time we're in Cabo San Lucas, Mexico. We've gotten a sweet deal on our condos through a work friend of Jeff's. One for us, one for the boys, and one for Brook and her friend.

When we walk into the resort, we see the main pool is being renovated.

"Oh darn, the pool is under construction," The kids whine in unison. "How will we survive without a pool?"

"I'm sure you'll enjoy the beach so much you won't miss the pool," I retort somewhat sarcastically. "Besides, there's a smaller pool close to the resort that you can swim in if you're desperate."

On our second day in Cabo, we plan to have dinner at a restaurant on the beach. We girls are all wearing our favorite sun dresses, and the boys wear whatever; we don't care. Girls dress up for each other anyway.

Tomorrow, we have reserved a half day of snorkeling on a catamaran cruise. From the beach we've been able to see people parasailing and renting jet skis. We want to do it all. Our blended family loves each other's company.

What a blessing.

✠ ✠ ✠

All our Cabo resort condos are adjacent to each other so that Becky and I can keep close tabs on the boys and girls. "Trust but verify" is going to be our motto on this vacation.

There are plenty of beach restaurants to choose from. "Let's just walk down the beach and pick one," I say to the gang.

Our server has leather ammo belts full of shot glasses criss-crossed on his chest, and he offers us cheap tequila from the bottles strapped inside his pistol holsters.

"That looks like fun, *señor*, but for us, *no gracias. Topo Chico, por favor*," I reply in my broken Spanish. Topo Chico sparkling water is Becky's and my go to drink.

The salsa is soupy, the Big Box guac is tasteless, the tortilla chips are stale and way too salty, the meat is tough and fatty, like the tequila server, and the mariachi band is beyond obnoxious—yet everyone is having an awesome time.

As we stroll back along the beach to our resort on this perfect moonlit night, I spot a group of men gathered maybe a hundred feet up from the waterline. Their cat calls break the peaceful night air. Brook is quickly enraged and abruptly turns toward them. She yells defiantly, "My dad is with us, and he will kick your ass!"

Oh, not good Brook, I think nervously. *Maybe they don't understand English, or even better, maybe they're too busy enjoying some cerveza.* I hear the ocean and nothing more. *This can't be good.* Then, a burst of laughter from our whistling amigos up the hill.

"Okay, family, just keep walking," I say with a huge sigh of relief.

Everyone is still talking about our encounter as we hurriedly head back to the resort.

"Sorry, I can't contribute to the conversation," I say in jest, but with a hint of truth. "I'm too busy looking over my shoulder for that gang of Cabo *hombres*."

✤ ✤ ✤

The teenage years are a time of testing boundaries. And boy, do they push the limit. We're dealing with a lot.

"What is this?" I (Becky) ask Jake, as he hands me a slip of paper.

"It's a ticket," he answers.

"What for? You don't even have a driver's license yet."

I soon learn that Jake and his buddies were skateboarding in the parking lot of one of the banks in town when the cops showed up.

I'm going to pass this problem on to his father.

"Go call your father and tell him what happened," I say. "Is there a court date on that ticket? You better ask your dad to go with you, because I'm not."

A couple weeks later, Jake and O.T. are at the courthouse.

"I'll let you get off with a two hundred dollar fine and a promise not to trespass again," says the judge from the bench.

"I promise," says Jake with a shaky voice.

As they are telling me the story after arriving home, I wonder how in the world Jake is going to pay that fine back to his dad.

✦ ✦ ✦

"Becky, you need to get over here now," I hear O.T. say on the other end of the line. "Jake has come home from school drunk."

I'm at work, but I tell them I have a family emergency and hit the road. My mind is going in circles, wondering how this could happen. As I pull into O.T.'s driveway Jack runs out of the house toward me.

"Mom, you should have seen Jake," Jack tells me. "He was acting like a stupid idiot on the bus, and then he tripped and rolled down the hill when he stepped off."

Oh my gosh, I've always dreaded that the kids would get in trouble with alcohol.

Knowing my own past, this has been one of my worst nightmares.

"Hello?" I say as I open the front door without knocking.

"We're upstairs in Jake's room. Come on up," O.T. answers.

As I enter the bedroom, I see Jake lying on his bed and O.T. sitting on the edge. His dad offers me a chair, which I accept.

"What happened?" I ask.

The answer is a story in itself.

"Apparently, our son has been skipping gym class with his buddy John," O.T. says. "They go over to John's house while his parents are at work. John's brother has been offering them vodka, thinking it's funny. After they are plenty drunk, the two boys return to school and somehow finish their last class. Then Jake comes home and voilà."

"My gosh, Jake, how long has this been going on?" I ask in shock. I know that high school has an open campus policy, which means the kids can leave the school grounds at will. But I'd had no idea this was happening.

"A couple of weeks," O.T. answers for him.

"Stay in your room until dinner," I say.

O.T. and I leave the room to discuss punishment.

We decide to ground Jake for a month, with no more open campus for him. He must sign up to work in the counselors' offices during his off period.

"And get rid of your friend John. He is bad news."

As far as this punishment is concerned, it all turns out well for Jake. He becomes the counselors' favorite student and eventually will receive nice recommendation letters from them when applying for college.

✠ ✠ ✠

Ding dong.

Who could that be on a Saturday morning? I wonder.

Uh oh, I think as I look through the front door windows and see two policemen.

I open the door reluctantly. "Hello. Can I help you?"

"Yes, ma'am. May we come in?"

I lead them inside to the kitchen where the rest of the family is gathered.

"Jake and Jack, go downstairs to your rooms," I say. They are only too happy to leave.

"Mrs. Atkinson, it appears your sons and their friends have been sneaking out at night and raising havoc on your neighbors. We found John's wallet on the street near one of the vandalized houses, and he gave us the other boys' names."

Not John again. We'll have to do something more about him.

The officers give us the addresses of the affected houses, and some information about the families. The worst damage was done to the house of a couple with two adopted, elementary school–aged daughters. There was toilet paper in the trees, eggs on the siding, and explicit words spray painted on the porch and sidewalk.

When we walk over to the house, I am flabbergasted.

My kids did this? Where did they learn those words? I feel so bad that those young girls are exposed to this.

The guilt is written all over the boys' down-turned faces.

"Let's get to work and clean this mess up," Jeff barks, as the other boys show up with their parents.

The second house is catty-corner from ours and belongs to one of the vice presidents at Jeff's company. The damage is a yard full of toilet paper and some eggs splattered on several windows. Jeff is both pissed off and embarrassed.

"Jack, get up," Jeff declares in the sternest voice I've ever heard him use as we return home. "We are going together to apologize to our neighbor, and you are going to do whatever it takes to make amends."

Our neighbor is surprisingly calm about the whole matter and brings his son out to meet Jeff and Jack.

"My son is about Jack's age, and I am very aware of how poor their judgment can be," he says sympathetically. "So, if Jack is available the next several weekends, I'll find some yardwork for him."

Jeff thanks him for being understanding.

"You can be certain Jack will make himself available, starting right now."

I get bored watching the cleanup and have run out of socially acceptable conversations with the other parents, so I head home, leaving Jeff to supervise.

What punishment can we come up with for Jake that will make a lasting impression? I wonder.

✤ ✤ ✤

Brook and Bryce both have moments of misbehavior as well. Their mom deals with most of it, usually without even informing me.

But right now, I'm the "Bad Dad."

When Brook talks about getting her license, I want her to prove she can be a responsible driver for six months before we get her a car. But Dad doesn't have the final say in this matter. Brook picks out her dream SUV and her mother purchases it, even though she only has her learner's permit.

Brook passes her driving exam flawlessly and begins driving herself to school.

It doesn't take long for peer pressure to trump the law, however. Brook is busted by her mom for driving a car full of teenage friends after school lets out for the day—something the state of Texas forbids when you are a new driver.

"Brook, your driving privileges are suspended for a month," her mom declares.

To her credit, Brook acknowledges her poor decision and becomes an amazingly responsible driver once her privileges are restored. Something good has come out of the bad. The "Wrath of Mom" makes Brook quickly forget I'm the "Bad Dad."

Will she ever see the wisdom in me having wanted her to prove she could be a responsible driver before owning a car? Maybe when she becomes a mom.

✢ ✢ ✢

Becky and I grew up in Christian households, but neither of us were strong in our faith in college and then into our twenties and thirties. We made a lot of poor choices. Fortunately, God's grace far outweighs any of our poor choices from those lost decades.

I suppose our faith journeys influenced why we didn't force our kids, once they were teenagers, to join us in worship and fellowship every Sunday. Good or bad, that's the decision Becky and I made together.

Knowing what we know now about the joy and strength of community with other believers, I wish we had made far more of an effort to expose our kids to regular worship and to church youth groups. But our faith has also taught us you can't "woulda coulda shoulda" our lives away. God's forgiveness offers renewal each day, so we ask for it and receive it. We also pray the foundation we laid when the kids were young will bring a renewing of their faith and relationship to God.

To this day, even as adults, the boys have never bombarded another crocodile sanctuary. Need more proof they have reformed? Odd has a doctorate in wildlife biology and spends much of his time studying monkeys in the jungles and forests of Central America. Atonement? Maybe.

Focusing on the behavior and not the person is hard, yet it was so crucial when calling out poor choices on the part of each of our children, especially as teenagers.

In the story of the adulterous woman Jesus says, "Has no one condemned you? ... Then, neither do I ... Go now and leave your life of sin" (John 8:3–11).

Christ did not condemn her, but He clearly did not condone her choice to commit adultery. In the same way, we did our best not to attack our children while still calling out behavior that was not acceptable.

"You are being punished for what you did, Bryce, and we know that's not who you really are. We don't love what you did, but our love for you is unconditional."

God says we are "fearfully and wonderfully made" (Psalm 139:14) We are made in His image yet with our own will to choose.

Our children's choices, good or bad, do not change the love God has for each of them, so they shouldn't dictate the degree to which we love them either.

"Go now and leave your life of sin"—and don't spray paint four-letter words on the neighbor's sidewalk anymore!

✢ ✢ ✢

My parents made me go to a non-denominational church through high school. I was made to go to Sunday school and sit through long, boring church services. I was also required to attend church on Wednesday evenings for Pioneer Girls, a sort of Christian Girl Scouts.

We also had some fun church activities, like a car wash, on Saturday afternoons. All in all, I spent about eight hours every week doing something either at or for the church. By the time I went to college, I had had enough church!

In college, I never went to church unless I was home. Through my adult years (before marrying Jeff) I experimented with other forms of so-called spirituality like crystals, astrology, and psychics. These things always led to disappointment.

I came full circle when Jeff and I started dating and were married. When I was in rehab for alcoholism, I gained a new appreciation for God, Jesus, and the Holy Spirit. Only they could keep me sober; I knew I couldn't do it alone.

Reflections on Our Story

—————JEFF—————

Whether it was not being able to hang out with certain people, not getting to participate in social occasions, working in the counselors' office at school during free period or being grounded for a while, in our family there were always consequences for inappropriate behavior.

Obviously, it wasn't all roses raising four teenagers. It was a lot of hard and sometimes painful work. We also needed to be in sync with the other parents, which meant a lot of communication with our exes.

The teenage years were all about the "Age of Accountability."

First, there was taking ownership for their lapses in judgment—a frequent event in our household. Second, there was taking ownership in their faith in God and Jesus Christ. We believed in giving each child the freedom to worship and to be in community with other Christian believers their age or not.

Brook embraced Christian community through Young Life. She especially loved the summer camping events in the mountains of Colorado. Sadly, as much as we continue to encourage and invite the boys, they are less interested in church. Whether their choice was due to their other parents, their peers, or both, it's hard to say.

Becky and I continue to attend and to serve our church, pray for our family, and believe they will one day be drawn back to the church.

———BECKY———

Each kid will be different from the others. Embrace *all* their strengths and weaknesses. Let them know you love them for who they are.

Go on family outings and vacations to new places. Vacations bring everyone together and create stories that everyone will remember for years to come.

Guess what? Your kids won't be perfect! They will get in trouble at times. Don't ignore bad behavior. Use consequences to teach them your values. With Jake, I had to deny him certain friendships that influenced his bad behavior. And of course, always discipline with love.

Keep encouraging your kids' relationships with God and Jesus. Sit down with them and share how important the relationship with the Divine has been in your own lives. Sometimes you must push a little to keep them participating in church and/or youth activities.

Get to know the youth pastors and introduce them to your kids. Don't just leave it up to them as teenagers (like we did) because most of the time they'll just stay in bed on Sunday mornings.

Questions for Discussion

Does your family spend quality time together? Do they enjoy doing activities together? What are some fun ways to add this to your family experiences?

_____

_____

_____

_____

Do you pray for help with raising your kids or do you depend solely on yourself and/or spouse?

_____

_____

_____

_____

What are some undesirable behaviors that your kids exhibit? Are there consequences? Can you think of other ways to discipline with love?

_____

_____

_____

_____

Are your children willing to freely discuss how they feel about God and Christ's church?

_____

_____

_____

_____

CHAPTER 4

BALANCING TWO CAREERS

O h man, I (Becky) wish I had more good things to say about my career choice. I am a Certified Public Accountant specializing in taxes. I've always worked for public accounting firms, first with the big ones and then with the smaller local firms.

It all began because I was good at math in school. My dad and I sat down one night to discuss my college major.

"I don't know what my major should be," I began, "much less which college to go to."

"I suggest accounting since you really enjoy and excel in math," offered my dad.

"I love you, Daddy, and I'm going to trust you on this one. Now, where should I go to college?"

I ended up attending Louisiana State University in Baton Rouge because a classmate of mine already went there and was having a blast. My best friend, Lucy, and I conspired together to convince our parents to let us go, and it worked.

I really liked my accounting courses until I took corporate tax my junior year. I was on my way to making a D, but somehow pulled out a C. This was after having a 4.0 in accounting up until that point. So, it makes no sense that I ended up working with income taxes.

My career consists of lots of ups and downs. I'm up when I'm busy and feel like I'm making a difference in the lives of my clients. I generally feel down and lackadaisical between tax filing dates when clients are nonresponsive to my questions and requests for further documentation.

One October fifteenth, the absolute last due date for individual tax returns on extension, I was still making calls to clients and waiting for approvals to file their returns until ten o'clock that evening. My bosses and I went over the due date control list about ten times that day. When we finally were convinced everything was done and filed, we left for home. It was midnight, and we had to be back at the office at eight the next morning.

It makes me crazy. I'm very stressed most of the time at work with either too much to do or nothing much at all. I bring my work stress home and complain a lot to the family. I'm not a great example to the kids, who have vowed to find careers doing something they love, rather than being miserable like Mom.

Ha, I guess some good has come out of it. Thank you, God.

✦ ✦ ✦

My first job after college paid the bills and that's about all it did. However, as I (Jeff) reflect, it did open the door to a career with one company lasting decades.

I have a Bachelor of Science degree in business administration, with a double major in marketing and management. I've spent the first six years after graduating in the world of advertising. I've learned how to listen, and I have become accustomed to the pressure of deadlines. Beyond that, I don't have much to say that's positive about marketing, and even worse, about where my adult life is heading.

At this point I'm twenty-eight years old, and I am ready for a new career. Thoughts of going to Navy flight school are starting to hang around in my heart.

Time to reach out to a Navy recruiter, I decide.

"Jeff, the officer candidate exam you took in college is still valid, but you'd better decide soon. The cutoff is twenty-eight years of age," the recruiter tells me.

Wow! That means now or never. How do I convince my wife, Mary, that a life in the service of our country is the right life for both of us?

Suddenly, haunting words from my mother-in-law begin to resurface. "You know, Jeff, you will never be able to take my daughter away from this family." A definitive statement from a protective mother, yet at the time, it meant nothing to me. But it sure does now.

Come on, Jeff, man up. That was six years ago. You've got to give this a try. Nothing ventured, nothing gained, right?

"Mary, I know you sense I am bored with advertising and that I need a real challenge," I tell her, having convinced myself that a short and direct statement is always best. "I want to join the Navy and go to flight school."

She is visibly shaken and almost in tears. Her reply comes straight out of her mother's book of unshakable truths. "Following you all over the world is not what I want or could ever do," she says. "I can never leave my family. You know they mean everything to me."

"I understand, Mary, and I'm sorry I upset you," I say, trying to soothe my wife. But for a guy who grew up in a military family, I'll never understand her feelings or have that same desire to plant roots. The grass will always be greener in the next career, next assignment, or next promotion, and I'll always look forward to it.

How else could she expect me to think if she really knew me?

The Navy will have to remain a dream for now, I tell myself as I wait for a racquetball court to open. *Thank goodness I have racquetball to blow off my frustration.*

I decide to strike up a conversation with the gentleman hanging out in the observation lounge to get my mind off my non-existent future, but he beats me to it.

"What do you do for a living?"

"I'm in advertising, print media, mostly. And you?"

"I'm the plant manager for a high-speed manufacturing facility here in town."

After fifteen minutes of casual conversation, my court is open, and we shake hands.

"It was a pleasure to meet you," I say. "Let me know if you ever want to play a match."

His reply catches me by surprise. "Why don't you come and tour our plant, Jeff," he says. "We have an opening for a shift supervisor, and your printing experience might make you a good fit."

I took Gene up on his offer, and it was the start of a thirty-nine-year career with the same company.

✢ ✢ ✢

Becky and I had not even been married for a year when a huge promotion opportunity was presented to me.

Dang, I hate to turn down a three-year assignment in Hong Kong, but how can I ask Becky to uproot when we have been married for only nine months?

Hmm, her job can be twenty-hour days during tax seasons. Maybe she would like the break from work? Plus, saying no could really slow my career advancement.

Geez, I am amazed how quickly my mind can turn from unselfish thoughts to just me, me, me. Nevertheless, at this point in my life, I could never be that far away from my kids. I decide to turn down the offer. *And I'm sticking to it—for now,* I tell myself.

Truth is, I love seeing my children every week and I don't want to become one of those absentee fathers, regardless of the title, the money, or the prestige that comes with the job offer. Plus, my stepsons' father deserves a close relationship with his young boys. Becky and I respect him far too much to deny them what every child needs at that age—a father.

✢ ✢ ✢

Moving to Colorado requires Jeff to take a demotion, but he takes it in stride because he knows it will lead to better advancement opportunities, plus he loves being back with his old engineering friends.

The downside to any future promotion means he will be required to travel farther and farther away from home. No longer is it just the United States, Canada, and Mexico. Promotions mean his travel will send him to South America, Central America, Europe, China, and Australia.

I know I will miss him a lot, and a part of me will probably be jealous of the places he is getting to visit, even if it is for work. No sense worrying about it too much, however, until those promotions happen.

✣ ✣ ✣

After three years back in Colorado, to say we both have demanding careers is an understatement. "Love you, see you Friday night," is becoming my routine Monday morning phrase these days. This new position requires a lot of travel, both foreign and domestic. The level of responsibility is closer to what I was used to in previous management positions, and I thrive on the added pressure to deliver positive results.

Titanium hotel status, platinum car rentals, and 1K mileage award upgrades are not something I'm striving for while climbing the corporate ladder—especially when it means Becky is quite often left parenting alone. Jake and Jack's father travels the "Friendly Skies" too, which really adds double to her weekly duties.

Becky deals with the added pressure of being a manager for a Certified Public Accounting firm specializing in corporate and personal taxes. It's not just her deadlines that have to be met but also those of the staff members reporting to her. Add single parenting on top of Becky's work role, and honestly, I don't know how she is able to do it all. She gets the kids out of bed and fed and on the school bus. She shuttles them to after-school activities, helps with homework, feeds them dinner, threatens video game privileges if they won't shower, and finally, gets them in bed at a reasonable hour—only to get up and do it again eight hours later. There's no conceivable way I could do that and do it well. Someone or something would be forgotten every day.

Becky truly is amazing when it comes to my work travel, or when I fly to Texas at the last minute to see Brook and Bryce. My being absent so much cannot be easy, but she never complains to me or hints that it's an issue.

There's a statue of Mother Cabrini we pass driving down the mountain toward Denver. It is an annual pilgrimage for Catholics in the Denver area. I'm going to sneak up there one night and change the plaque to read "Mother Rebecca."

✣ ✣ ✣

One by one, year by year, each kid starts attending college. None of them make the choice to do otherwise. Financially, it's a big challenge with four kids in college at the same time. My boys have a trust fund set up by their grandparents to pay for most of college. We are paying the rest out of Jeff's 401(k), bonuses, and our savings. None of the kids will leave school with debt.

We aren't experiencing much loss or loneliness because we are busy living our own lives. We have never found ourselves living vicariously through our kids. We have done our best to raise them right, and now we need to trust we did a good job. I also trust that God will watch over them and keep them out of harm's way.

✣ ✣ ✣

We've finally made it to the college years, and it starts with Brook. The drive to Ft. Collins and Brook's freshman dorm at Colorado State University is one of excitement for her and full of logistics for me. *How are we going to get all these boxes and storage bins up to the second floor and then, find places for all her "can't live without" items in such a small space Brook must share with another freshman?*

The hauling boxes part is quickly solved by six male students more than eager for a shot at a first date with a beautiful eighteen-year-old.

As for the storage and arrangement part, I relinquish control with these words: "Well, Apple, we are leaving that challenge to you and your roommate to figure out." We share a goodbye hug, and I slip an extra one hundred dollars into her hand.

Neither of us experiences the hollowness parents feel on that long drive back home.

Surprisingly, we never experience that emptiness with any of our freshman children. We are excited for them, and for us. Heading off to college is a rite of passage, and I start their cross-over from "minor hood" to adulthood with my "you're now eighteen, and, in our eyes, an adult" speech.

"Bryce, now that you are going to college, you get to make your own decisions, including premarital sex or not, alcohol or not, smoking or not, studying or not, sleeping or not, and eating Taco Bell and Chipotle five nights a week or not." (Taco Bell is the official sponsor of the "freshman fifteen.")

"Jake, you are also now responsible for the consequences of your actions based upon your decisions. Please keep this in mind. Not every decision you make will have our blessing, nor our financial support, but they are your choices to freely make."

✠ ✠ ✠

Brook is home for the weekend. We are so glad she chose to attend college in Colorado. I don't even mind her bringing six loads of laundry with her.

"Where on earth did she find space in that tiny dorm room for all those dirty clothes?" Becky whispers to me as we unload Brook's Hummer.

"Brook, I promised to donate blood today, would you like to give also?" I ask her.

"Sure."

"Super, first you'll need to answer a few questions from the blood bank."

I call up the blood bank, hand the phone over to Brook, and listen as she responds, "No, no, no, no, ahh… yyyes, thank you," and hangs up.

"I can't give blood, Dad. I have a tattoo, and I haven't had it a year," she shyly tells me.

Expecting a What-Were-You-Thinking lecture from me, I look at her, and in a calm voice I ask, "Are you eighteen?"

The tattoo is cool too. It's an *ichthus*, the fish symbol for Christianity.

✤ ✤ ✤

We are seven-plus years into our sobriety, three kids are in college, the youngest is one semester away from matriculating, and the title of Empty Nesters is soon to be ours for the taking.

I spend the summer and fall of 2012 in Brazil, working with our South American manufacturing division's engineering team. The assignment is to observe, then make recommendations for an independent department of engineering, reporting directly to the South American president of operations.

In November 2012, I present my detailed recommendations to the president.

He says, "This all looks great. Do you want to be the first Director of Engineering in South America for the next three years?"

After talking it over with Becky, I accept the offer.

My new boss responds, "Perfect, and by the way, I'm leaving in January to be the president of our European operations. Here are the keys to $100 million in capital projects."

✢ ✢ ✢

Jack, my youngest, is about to start his last semester of high school. We are dumping him at his dad's and moving to Brazil (ha-ha). No really, we kinda are. Jeff has accepted the new position of Director of Engineering for his company's South American operations headquartered in Brazil. It is a great opportunity for Jeff, and exciting for me. I just need to break the news to Jack.

"Jack, please sit down," I say. "You're not in trouble. We have something to discuss with you." Jack looks at me wide-eyed. *I hope he's not going to be upset.* I continue, "Jeff has accepted an overseas assignment in Brazil, and he and I are moving there. This means you will be living full time with your dad." (All the other kids are living at college by this point.)

"No problem," he replies. (Such a sweet kid!)

So, I tell my office that I'm taking a break from work. My boss promises to hire me back when we return to Colorado.

Work visas and temporary resident visas in hand and seven suitcases packed, we head for the Denver airport on January 2, 2013, and to our new home in Brazil—so we think.

What we didn't get communicated to us was Brazil's Customs Agency changed their luggage policy on their official website the day before. Now, only three suitcases are allowed per person to enter the country.

Back to the Colorado house we go, and the stress level builds as we take inventory of everything we packed.

"Bec, I can live without my electric razor, but not without my iPod."

"Jeff, I can live without two of my dresses, but not without six bikinis."

"Bec, I can live without the Keurig coffee maker, but not without the pour over."

"Jeff, I can live without my ten Pilates shorts, but not without my twelve Pilates pants and sport bras"

"Bec, I'll take the flat screen monitor as carry-on in my garment bag."

Okay, one less suitcase, check. Sanity restored, check. Let's fly to São Paulo, Brazil!

The next day, we begin apartment shopping.

"I think this one is the one, honey. It's huge and has enough bedrooms and baths for each of the kids when they visit at Christmas. And look at this large terrace overlooking the park across the street."

"Yeah, I like it too," Jeff replies.

We really love this place. It has cool tiles, a quaint kitchen, a small private TV room (where I spend most evenings), and a large master bath. We are close to the mall, the grocery store, and lots of small coffee shops/cafés that we frequent, especially on weekend afternoons. They are places where Jeff and I reconnect and focus on each other.

I don't have a car (Jeff does), so I walk just about everywhere I go.

Jeff still travels a lot with his new position, so I'm left alone Mondays through Fridays. I'm doing fine, though. I have leisurely mornings, work out at a state-of-the-art gym behind our apartment building, take tennis lessons at Club de Campo Santa Rita, and walk to the grocery store every few days because I can only carry what fits in my backpack.

I also meet with a group of ex-pat women whose husbands have also been assigned to Brazil at least twice a month for coffee and conversation. It's fun and interesting to meet women from all over the world.

Three times a week I have Portuguese lessons in the afternoons. *"Claro! Claro!"* I say loudly as I pretend to leave and enter the front door. My teacher is having me practice greeting people. I feel ridiculous.

Late in the day I visit one of the local coffee shops for an espresso and some food to take back to the apartment for my dinner. At nighttime I hunker down in the TV room to eat dinner and binge-watch Netflix. Sometimes I stay up until the wee hours of the morning.

We even have a maid come once a week. There's a washer but no dryer. On wash day sheets and towels are thrown all over the furniture in the living and dining rooms to air dry. Luckily, they should be dry by late afternoon.

Many weekends Jeff and I venture out in search of one of the beautiful beaches surrounding us. But literally every time we arrive at a beach it rains buckets on us. One Saturday was particularly irritating.

"Oh my gosh, Jeff. When will this traffic clear up?"

"Maybe never. I forgot it's a holiday weekend and everyone appears to be on their way home."

Six hours later (for what should have been a ninety-minute drive) we finally arrive at the apartment. We never fought, yelled at each other, or got upset. We just focused on the common enemy: the horrible traffic.

✣ ✣ ✣

Thanks to our South American division's fantastic HR and administrative team, we settle into our new surroundings and my assignment with few issues. My commute to work is less than twenty minutes. The Garmin GPS my team back in Colorado gave me as a going-away gift is a godsend. We can walk to restaurants, the gym, and most importantly, the cafés! Quickly, our favorite coffee shop becomes the one just around the corner from the apartment.

"Becky, I must introduce you to pão de queijo. It's Brazilian cheese bread shaped in round, puffy balls. Oh so, so good." Becky immediately falls in love with pão de queijo and asks the café owner for her recipe. The owner laughs, goes back to the kitchen and returns with a giant Sam's Club bag of frozen pão de queijo.

My engineering team, the plant manager, and the plant staff have made us feel welcomed from day one.

There are two requirements when you first arrive in Brazil. First, you MUST pick a professional soccer team to root for, preferably, one of the four teams in São Paulo, Brazil. I pick a team, and then I am immediately chastised by fans of the other three teams in São Paulo.

"Palmeiras??? Why would you root for the 'PIGS'???!!!"

The second requirement is you must be ready to barbecue at every opportunity, and there are many. It seems everyone has an elaborate barbecue setup, including us. Our balcony features a gourmet grill and kitchen.

What is a typical barbecue like? You arrive at 7:00 p.m., which means anytime between 7:00 and 8:00 p.m. The grilled buffalo cheese, bread, and meats are served for the next five hours. Then, at 1:00 a.m. you begin enjoying desserts and espressos. Finally, at 2:00 a.m., you say "*obrigado*" and "*chao*" to your lovely hosts before heading home, wishing you had worn sweatpants to the party.

Our new president, my boss, is from England. He is sharp, with lots of international experience, and always ready to dig in and help solve complex problems. And he speaks English, a language I mistakenly think I am fluent in. His accent is so heavy I need subtitles to understand him. He is a Manchester City football (soccer) fan through and through. He hates Arsenal's football team with a passion and constantly makes derogatory comments about the "Gooners." Three months into working with him my daughter's boyfriend tells me Arsenal's team name is the "Gunners, not Gooners." I'm going to need a translator to go along with the subtitles, but not just for me. In group presentations to the boss, my team comes up to me and says, "We understand your English, Jeff, but the president's English we never learned in school."

Major capital projects in four different manufacturing plants scattered over Brazil keep me on the road often. Thankfully, São Jose dos Campos is the safest city in all of Brazil, so I feel comfortable leaving Becky at home by herself. Plus, she has an incredible Portuguese language instructor, Carla, who is always available to help her navigate a taxi ride, a nail appointment, or a trip to the mall.

I can picture Carla replying with her wonderful Brazilian accent, "*Claro*, sure, I'll help you, Becky."

I'm always home for the weekends. Saturdays are usually exploration days and Sundays are church and tennis days.

My electrical engineer invited us to his Evangelical Baptist church, and it is becoming our regular church home. The services are in Portuguese, but there are enough ex-pats and English-speaking members to help us better understand the sermons. The worship music is modern with a Brazilian flair that makes you want to dance. As is always the case with mega churches, getting out of the parking lot is an exercise in godly patience.

✤ ✤ ✤

I love living in São Jose do Campos, but I hardly ever get to travel outside of the city. I get to visit São Paolo, the largest and most dangerous city in Brazil, a couple times for brunch or lunch with Jeff's work colleagues. No Rio de Janeiro for Becky. But Jeff goes there many times.

The first time he went, I remembered his call after work.

"Hello," I answer the phone.

"Hi, sweetie. Man, it's been a long day."

"I'm sorry. What are you doing now?"

"I'm out on my hotel balcony looking at all the women in skimpy bikinis. Some don't have tops on. It's fascinating," Jeff says.

"You're hilarious. I want to visit Rio too," I whine.

I know he is teasing me, but I don't mind. My trust in him is as complete as my trust in Christ.

✢ ✢ ✢

Just as I am hitting my stride with the engineering team and projects, my boss calls me out of the blue and tells me our corporation is creating a global team to oversee all regional operations, and I should expect a call from the newly appointed President of Global Operations. My mind races.

Wow, just nine months into our three-year assignment. This is not something I was expecting.

The call comes as I am driving to work. All I remember is saying, "Yes, I'd be honored to be a part of your leadership team."

My new headquarters will be in Zurich, Switzerland, but I am allowed to return to Colorado and make it my home base. So, with six lighter suitcases, Becky and I head back to our mountain home in October of 2013.

✢ ✢ ✢

Nine months go by quickly. Our kids never had a chance to come visit. That big apartment was all for naught.

I particularly get scolded by my oldest son, Jake, for leaving Brazil. He had wanted so badly to go to Brazil the next summer when the World Cup was being played in São Paolo. We tried so hard to make it work for him staying with friends, but nothing panned out.

"Jake, you've got to get over not going to the World Cup," I beg.

"Never! I can't believe you are leaving Brazil already." I can hear Jake stomping around his apartment.

But of course, he finally forgave me, eventually. It took him quite a while to do so.

The company gave Jeff some time off after his assignment, and we decided to vacation on the eco-island of Fernando de Noronha, famous for its beaches and lagoons. However, true to our bad luck with beaches in Brazil, the weather forecast was rain on the island throughout our planned stay. So, we cancel our reservation and fly to Iguazu Falls, the famous waterfalls on the border of Brazil and Argentina.

Well, what do you know, we arrive and it's raining buckets. The rain continues every day we're there. Such a disappointing end to our time in Brazil.

Back in Colorado, Jeff is starting his new position. Guess where his first travel assignment is? Zurich, Switzerland! I am so excited!

Then Jeff says, "You can't go. I will be in meetings and working dinners and won't have time to do anything with you. You will be stuck in a hotel room."

"So, I don't mind. I'll venture around by myself during the day. I'm not afraid. Then I'll order a nice dinner from room service."

"Bec, please don't go. It'd be too distracting for me. I have a lot of important work to do there."

"Okay," I pout.

Jeff and I don't yell or fight over my not going to Zurich with him. I let him know I was deeply disappointed, but I learn to leave his career decisions up to him. And he expresses his gratitude for me.

When a girlfriend tells me about a chick trip to the Italian Riviera, I sign up so fast Jeff didn't have any say so. I feel totally justified.

+ + +

It's true my time is packed with meetings and dinners in Zurich. Every night I return late to a five-by-eight-foot cell in a five-hundred-dollar-a-night boutique hotel room. Then I take a shower in a space so small I bruise my elbows while shampooing. As I rub my sore elbows, I think, *I understand now why Europeans never seem to be fat.*

Any sense of guilt for not bringing Becky to Zurich totally vanishes after we Skype, and she shows me her panoramic view of the Tuscan wine country from the balcony of her cavernous suite in Italy.

+ + +

I know it sounds crazy, but I've decided to go back to work part-time. It helps fill my time while Jeff is jet-setting around the globe, plus it gives me a little money of my own. (You know the saying: *Your money is our money, my money is my money,* hee hee.)

Summer is coming and I'm feeling bored at work. *I think I need a vacation.*

"Honey, I'm feeling restless, and work is so slow this time of year," I tell Jeff. "Let's take a few days and go somewhere new."

Jeff answers, "Let me check my work travel schedule and see if I have a break coming up. Yeah, we could go in June, I think. Where would you like to go?"

"Dunno, somewhere warm and close to the beach."

"How about California? Let me check my American Express travel rewards."

We decided on a resort near La Jolla, California, a beautiful cliffside town just north of San Diego. We have a great time walking the beaches, hiking in the cliffs overlooking the ocean, shopping in La Jolla, and eating delicious food. We also relax by the pool, which is one of my favorite activities.

It's important for couples to go on holiday together, whether it's to another state or camping at a local park. It's a great break from everyday life and gives us new experiences to share.

✛ ✛ ✛

Jeff's mom, Pat, who is in her nineties and lives in Pennsylvania, has been getting feebler and lonelier since his father, Roy, passed away a couple of years ago. Jeff, always the good son, calls her every evening.

"Bec, Mom is making noises about moving to Colorado to be close to us. What do you think?"

"Well, I hate for her to sell her house and move here and hate it, missing all her friends in Mechanicsburg. But I sure can't blame her for wanting to be around you all the time."

"Maybe she could come for a long visit and test out the waters. How does that sound?"

"I'd love to have her," I say with a grimace, "but tax season is around the corner. With all your travel, it's going to really stress me out to take care of her too."

"I'm sure it will all work out." (Jeff says this about everything). "I'll make reservations to fly up and get her and bring her here."

Famous last words, I think as I roll my eyes.

Pat stays upstairs in our guest room. We put a TV in her room, bring her meals upstairs, and frequently go up to visit. Just as the tax deadline approached, Jeff left for a leadership meeting in Europe. I just about lost it taking care of her and working a hard deadline. I prayed daily for patience.

One day I found myself crying tears of desperation. Somehow, through God's grace, I come out the other side without hurting my relationships with Pat or Jeff. However, I do have a serious discussion when Jeff returns home.

"Please don't ask me to take care of your mom, or anyone else, during tax season. You know how seriously I take my job."

"I know, honey, and I'm sorry. It won't happen again. I love you," Jeff responds.

"I love you too, and I love your mom."

It's important to talk through bad times and say you're sorry when in the wrong. Otherwise, the bad feelings will gnaw at your heart.

Later, Pat begins to experience altitude sickness. We move her down the mountain to Golden and set her up in a Residence Inn suite. Jeff calls her a few times a day, and we bring dinner to her room and eat with her. After visiting a while after dinner, we would leave to go home and feel guilty.

She continues to have bad headaches and gets weaker, so we eventually move her back to Pennsylvania. Thank goodness we didn't sell her home.

✢ ✢ ✢

Jeff's mom decides after just two months that Colorado is not good for her health, so she flies back home to the East Coast. Jeff and I love to travel with each other, so after she leaves, we begin to travel by car to places in Colorado we always wanted to visit.

First, we drive toward Colorado Springs and visit the Garden of the Gods and climb the Incline, a hiking trail rising a mile straight up the mountain above Manitou Springs. It has uneven steps built from old railroad ties. (Believe me, it's a challenging climb.) We go on lots of hikes together, including to the top of Mt. Evans, which still has snow on the top in July 2018. We enjoy long walks around the hilly streets of our neighborhood while talking about our future together. At the end of the spring ski season, we drive to Beaver Creek to take our last ski runs. Jeff is a better skier by far, but for once I was looking forward to having a fun time skiing. Usually, I'm petrified of falling off the mountain.

Our kids come home at times, and we really enjoy spending time with our adult kids. We usually talk, laugh, and reminisce about all our fun family times and vacations together.

You see, all the hard work raising kids has been so worth it!

✦ ✦ ✦

It's October and our global team is meeting in Berlin, Germany, to make a presentation to the board of directors today. My part is to cover efforts to standardize engineering and operational practices globally, along with promising new technologies.

That went better than expected, I think after my presentation is finished. *Okay, knees, you can stop knocking anytime now.*

I listen to the regional presidents make their pitch for new capital project funding. I'm really looking forward to hearing about the North America project for Mexico. The capital request is for a mega plant in Monterrey, Mexico, that will feature the latest in manufacturing technology, including robotics and real-time process monitoring. It will require importing many direct and indirect process manufacturing materials, all carefully tracked and monitored by local, state, and national government regulators, who love documentation and live for opportunities to find discrepancies. The plant will be staffed by talent from Mexico and a plant manager initially from within our corporation, with the goal of eventually turning the reins over to someone native to Mexico.

Not surprisingly, the board approves the Monterrey project. I approach the North American president and offer my assistance. I had directed technical support for our former licensee in Mexico and am very familiar with the work ethic, level of experience, and leadership talent potentially available to us.

Three weeks after the board meeting, my global boss, now living in Colorado, calls me into his office and asks if I want to be the first plant manager of our Monterrey plant. Obviously, I want to talk to Becky first, but there is no doubt in my mind I want that job! I love the Mexican culture, and I truly believe individuals from Mexico, who I worked with in the past and greatly respect, will want to share this incredible opportunity with me.

Becky says yes, and so it's off to Mexico for another great assignment together.

✠ ✠ ✠

Getting the position of plant manager at the new state-of-the-art plant in Monterrey is a big deal for Jeff. We move to San Pedro Garza García, Mexico, an affluent city close to Monterrey. San Pedro has much less crime than the big city of Monterrey, so after Jeff's corporate security vetted multiple locations within the city, they set us up in an apartment. This time our apartment is on the nineteenth floor of a high-rise building. It's smaller than the apartment in Brazil but ultra-modern and beautiful. Our balcony looks down on the luxurious pool, complete with a huge waterfall and surrounded by pergolas and grilling areas. We are across a busy street from the new mall, and there are many fun and delicious restaurants.

In the early months, while the plant is under construction, Jeff interviews candidates from Mexico for managerial level positions, including an assistant plant manager. Almost every night we take interviewees out to delicious restaurants. It's a lot of fun dressing up and socializing with our new friends.

Once all the people are hired, the plant is ready to start production. Now the fancy dinners happen only when someone important visits from corporate. Jeff's hard work starts, and I am pretty much left to entertain myself.

✠ ✠ ✠

When I arrive in Mexico to begin hiring, the first and most important decision is to pick a professional soccer team to cheer for, and to wear their colors. (Sound familiar?) The choices are either the Monterrey Rayados or the Monterrey Tigres. *Vamos, Tigres!* I like the uniforms.

By May 2015, with the aid of many incredible individuals, and the worldwide reputation of our corporation, we have our management team hired and in place. We have assembled a team with the drive, the leadership, and the work ethic to build something very special, and they are bringing with them talented, experienced subordinates who also embrace our vision, even knowing the hard work and the challenges that lay ahead for the next two years.

Mid-May, the managers and I fly up to Colorado for orientation and training with the individuals who will support their departments. The Colorado weather in May can be unbelievably beautiful, or it can be unbelievably bad. It decides to be the latter: cold, misty, windy, and miserable. Sounds like perfect weather for a baseball game.

Harsh elements seldom stop the Colorado Rockies from playing ball, so after purchasing black Rockies parkas and purple hoodies, the Monterrey managers, their newfound colleagues, and I are off to see a night baseball game.

This is truly a fun night, even with our teeth chattering, I think.

I hear the crack of a bat and see a foul ball heading our way. One of the Monterrey managers quickly reacts and catches the foul ball sent screaming in our direction from one of the San Francisco players. A Giants fan quickly approaches him and asks if he would mind giving her the foul ball.

"No, my son likes baseball, and I want it for him," he replies.

She continues her plea, sounding more desperate.

"Please, Brandon Belt is my favorite player of all time, I must have that baseball. I'll give you a hundred dollars for it," she begs.

But the souvenir ball travels back with us to Monterrey, Mexico. A smiling son, priceless.

✢ ✢ ✢

Tomorrow, we start up our first of many manufacturing lines, but tonight we celebrate the hard work that got us to this point. What better way than to watch the Denver Broncos take on the

Carolina Panthers at Chili's. We have reserved the bar area for the plant management team, their wives, our great support group from the United States, and Becky and me, "*el jefe*." It's the perfect way to build momentum for the following day and the weeks to come. Lots of Denver fans are at Chili's tonight, and the Broncos don't disappoint with a final score of 24-10.

Start-ups are always a grind, but we have a solid core of plant leadership, project managers, and crew members who get the manufacturing lines up and operational in exceptional time.

✤ ✤ ✤

My schedule here isn't much different from Brazil. I go to yoga a couple mornings a week, work out with a trainer in the gym at the apartments, take tennis lessons, lay out at the pool, and have lunch once a week with the spouses of the managers at the plant. I frequently walk to the grocery store with my backpack. I also enjoy shopping at the fancy mall across the street from our apartment.

Jeff's "guys" from work organize barbecues with delicious cheeses and meats and beer (we drink Topo Chico) for their friends and families and include us. We really enjoy these barbecues!

Jeff and I see each other at the end of the day, usually around 9 p.m. Our go-to late-night dinner is a ham and cheese croissant or grilled cheese and coffee at Starbucks on the ground level of our apartment building. We like to finish it off with red velvet cake or a chocolate chip cookie. We relax and talk about our day before going back up the elevator for the evening.

For Jeff, the night doesn't end there. He is constantly being pulled toward work. The texts and phone calls are nonstop.

Sometimes he wakes up at around 3 a.m. to go back into the plant to solve a problem. He is always so exhausted.

I try not to complain but be supportive.

He does not need the additional stress of worrying about me.

✤ ✤ ✤

Early into the Monterrey plant's start-up I learn that we have plans to build another plant in Mexico, and I am asked to be ready in 2017 to help support that project. Becky is very enthusiastic about this next assignment, probably because it will get her within driving distance of the Baja beaches.

Can't think too much about that project. I have enough on my plate with this one.

After the US election in 2016, we learn that the new project is being placed on hold, due in part to the uncertain political atmosphere between the US and Mexico going into the New Year. Becky and I are then told we will be reassigned back to Colorado in February 2017.

✤ ✤ ✤

I continued to work part-time after we returned to Colorado. Finally, it's my last tax season; I'm so excited. After the April 2018 tax season, I will finally be retiring from a career I hated (most of the time).

What am I going to do with myself? I wonder. *I need to do something to feel useful.*

One day as I'm scrolling on Facebook, I see a guru talking about life coaching. I have secretly always wanted to be a psychologist, and a life coach seems like the closest thing without having to go back to school. I sign up for his online course, but it leaves me with more questions than answers.

I think I'll investigate some live life coaching courses.

"Jeff, I've been thinking of becoming a life coach," I say one day after he comes downstairs after work. (This was during Covid when everyone worked from home.) "What do you think?" I ask with some trepidation.

"What's a life coach?"

"It's like being a guide to people going through a life crises or change. They don't want therapy but need some help."

"Oh, okay. How do you get qualified to become this guide?"

I thought he'd never ask.

"Well, I've been doing some research and found a five-day immersion course in San Diego."

"San Diego? Honey, I can't take off from work right now."

"I'll go by myself. It's in the program leader's home and you end the five days as a certified life coach."

I sign up, buy an airplane ticket, and make reservations at a nearby hotel. The course is taught by a real life coach who graduated years ago and has many years of experience.

There are about ten of us, mostly females, in the group that week. We all get along well and pair off quite a bit to practice life coaching each other. This gives us a real taste of what to do, say, and expect from our clients. I study at night, reading and writing in my workbook. The end of the week finally arrives along with comprehensive tests. Our certification awards were soon mailed to us.

Back home, I don't know how to start, so I hire my course's teacher as my life coach. She coaches me for about six weeks over the phone, giving me more confidence and helping me become aware of my feelings.

The biggest problem I have is marketing and promoting myself. I set up a coaching "retreat" in Jack's old room in the basement. I join the chamber of commerce, advertise in the community magazine, and post almost every day on Facebook. Finally, the phone rings.

"Hello. This is Becky."

"Is this Becky, the life coach?" a woman asks.

"Yes. Can I help you in some way?"

"My husband saw your article in an Evergreen magazine and suggested I call you. You see, I've been trying to lose weight and have reached my wit's end."

"I believe I can help with that. How much weight are you wanting to lose?"

"Fifteen pounds."

I sign her up. *Yippee, my first client.*

My program is six weeks of weekly in-person hourlong coaching sessions and some phone calls during which I share some tips and tricks. She loses those burdensome fifteen pounds and wants to renew her contract at the same price. I'd been coached to increase my prices if this happened. So, despite my better judgment and comfort level, I increase my fee. Of course, she says no and that was it.

It is over; see ya never.

I decide to move my "retreat" out of the house to a small and cozy office space down the street from our neighborhood. Literally takes two minutes to drive to it. *Build it and the clients will come*, or so I think. Jeff helps me set up the space very nicely with a small couch, comfy chair, some tables, lamps, and a desk.

I get another client. An older woman comes to see me with her adult son. She complains of anxiety. Her son approves of me, and I begin coaching her with weekly in-person hourly sessions. We talk a lot about her discomfort in social situations, and I help her learn to cope, teaching her some tips and tricks I had learned. At the end of our contract, she feels much better and does not renew.

I don't receive any calls for over a month. Continuing to advertise seems like a waste of money, and I never got referrals from the women in the clubs I had joined. So, I close the business. The good thing about this experience is that I received a lot of life coaching for myself and therefore grew in my personal life. I'm more secure within myself and learn to be myself.

Jeff supports me all the way, even my decision to quit. He's the love of my life and my rock.

✙ ✙ ✙

My sixtieth birthday is coming up soon, and we decide to go back to Cabo, Mexico, just the two of us this time. We stay at a "beachy" apartment close to the harbor. The beach is a block away as well as lots of restaurants. We eat at Ruth's Chris Steak House on the water for my birthday, and another restaurant three nights in a row. Can you guess it was our favorite restaurant? You can go to the same restaurant night after night when there are no kids to please.

✙ ✙ ✙

Back home, I'm soon having lunch with a good friend at a local restaurant. "Tell me about the book you've written," I ask.

"Oh, it's a children's book about Jesus."

"Was it hard to write? How did you get it published?"

"Here's the name and number of the man who helped me with everything."

I call her contact and after talking with him about my idea, I decide to write and publish a memoir about my experiences with alcoholism and how I stayed sober. I call the book *I Drink, Therefore I Am*. I spend about six months writing it. After it was published, I have a book signing party at a local bookstore where I give a short speech to a crowded room. I sell a few books but mostly give out copies to family and friends. The experience gives me closure to that part of my life.

Reflections on Our Story

BECKY

When possible, put your relationship with your family and spouse before your job. As you'll see in the following chapters, the job eventually ends, but your relationship with your family lasts a lifetime. Neither Jeff nor I were good at this, but we discovered after retiring that our jobs weren't as important as we thought.

Support and respect your spouse's career choices, especially when they're the primary breadwinner. (I'll probably get a lot of grief for that statement.) But it's also important to discuss each of your career developments and be sure both of you are on board with the ultimate choices. Change is almost always hard, but new opportunities can be exciting and lead to growth in your relationship.

Kids will most likely leave the house after high school—either for college, a job, to live with friends, or a combination of these. Let them go and learn to be adults and take care of themselves. Try not to be a "helicopter" parent, calling several times a day to check on them. You must trust that you raised them the best you knew how, and now it is time for God to take over. Try new things that interest you. Even if it doesn't work out as planned, you will probably be empowered through the experiences.

———JEFF———

Looking back, I never made a conscious decision to avoid travel. Even when Becky was in rehab, I would have traveled if needed.

I interviewed for a director's level position that would have taken me all over the globe, and that was just three weeks into Becky's sobriety. How unbelievable that I'd even consider such a position at a critical time in Becky's recovery, but that was my career-oriented mindset, most of the time.

Fortunately, a dear friend was awarded the job, saving me from not being there for Becky had I been offered the position. No doubt that would have been the final nail in the coffin of our fragile marriage. God's intervention? For sure!

If you have worked for the same company for as long as I did, your career is bound to ebb and flow. My first ebb, a demotion, placed me back with the same group I had managed prior to moving from Colorado to Texas.

I was not in a good place with my Texas boss. I wanted to run my department, and so did he. It was impacting me mentally and physically, and I needed to move on, even if it meant taking a step or two back in my career. In the corporate world, I often find it takes just one person, one boss, to get your career back on track. I was fortunate to have several rooting for me over the years, and their timing was impeccable, always just when I truly needed encouragement and recognition.

As the saying goes, when walking through the manure in the cow pasture, just keep on walking. The twenty-third Psalm speaks to the same difficult times in our lives and reminds us God is there beside us giving us comfort and a positive attitude. Just what we need to push on through the challenging times.

The Monterrey plant had its share of "walk through the valley of the shadow of death" moments, mostly because of the unknowns you didn't have time to plan for: a stolen shipment, power outages and restrictions, dormant insects that hatch only after tropical storms, and material delays at the border to name a few. 1 Thessalonians 5:18 says to "Give thanks in all circumstances; for this is God's will for you in Christ Jesus." In 2016, I flat wore out that verse. I give glory to God for guiding me and my management team through all the challenges, and today I am proud to say many of those managers now lead their own manufacturing plants.

Becky and I both went to college in the seventies and have lots of firsthand knowledge of the temptations eighteen-year-olds will be exposed to—probably as early as the first night away from home. We prayed they would have the discernment and the strength to not follow the wild ones. I'm especially referring to the guy who jumps off the third-story balcony and plunges into the student housing apartment pool just to win the communal beer bong—if or when he surfaces.

Did we expect them to be perfect? Of course not, but we did hope, just like most loving parents, that they would do better in the common sense department than we ever displayed at their age.

Did we worry about them? Absolutely! Were we inquisitive at times? Certainly! But not to the level of being intrusive into their adult lives.

One positive memory from our kids' college years was how much better the conversations were when they returned home for the holidays. The days of one-word replies were gone. They were replaced by fully composed sentences, hourlong conversations, adult jokes, laughter, and a genuine desire to hang around the dinner table together. We somehow always gravitated to the kitchen when we were tired of sitting.

Thought... a fourth-year behavioral science major should write a thesis on "Why kitchens are always the social gathering spot of choice."

Questions for Discussion

Do you and your spouse have stressful careers along with raising a family? How do you handle these two things?

_____

_____

_____

_____

Are you stuck in the mud and bored with life? What are some activities that interest you that you can add into your lives?

_____

_____

_____

_____

Has there been a significant change in your daily lives? How do you handle big decisions together?

_____

_____

_____

_____

Has one of you had to make big compromises for the other? How does that make you feel, and have you talked about those feelings with one another?

_____

_____

_____

_____

At what age do you see your children as adults? How are your relationships with your adult children? Do you enjoy each other's company or avoid each other? What are some ways you can re-connect with your family?

_____

_____

_____

_____

CHAPTER 5

YOU HAVE CANCER

W hile the Monterrey plant is still under construction, I discover an unusual bump on the right side of my head, just behind my right ear. It is constantly irritated by the plastic suspension system in the construction hard hat I wear every day, and it annoys me for nine months until, finally, in April 2016, I meet with my dermatologist, Dr. Marina. After a visual exam she tells me she thinks it's a cyst.

"I don't have a lot of free time to come back on another day. Can you remove it in your office, now?" I ask more as a command than a request. After all, I had a huge plant to get up and running, and as they say, time is money and money is time.

"Yes, we can excise it here under local anesthesia."

"Great, let's get this done!"

The expression on the doctor's face, as she struggles to remove the mass, tells me it is more than a cyst.

"I need to send this to the lab," she says.

Since I spent much of my twenties and thirties on the water and out in the sun, my white, European heritage skin has become a fertile breeding ground for basal-cell carcinoma. I've had some small cancerous lesions removed before where the biopsy confirms basal cell; they cut out the cancer in the doctor's office; stitch me up; tell me over the phone that the margins are clean and end the call with "See you in six months for another check-up." This time, however, the doctor's tone is different. It doesn't sound like it's going to be business as usual.

A few days go by, and there's a note from my plant administrative assistant to contact Dr. Marina.

"Jeff, I have the results from the biopsy. Can you come into my office today? It is best we talk in person."

"Yes, late this afternoon, say *dieciséis horas?*"

"Yes, four o'clock will be fine."

+ + +

"Jeff, thank you for coming in today," Dr. Marina says that afternoon. "I prefer not to discuss lab results over the phone, especially in this instance. The diagnosis is angiosarcoma, a rare type of vascular cancer. The scalp is a common area where this cancer can develop. I am going to refer you to Dr. Martinez. He is a very good oncologist here in Monterrey. It is best you see him soon."

"Thank you, doctor, I'll contact him immediately."

Damn, I sensed it might be different this time, but I wasn't expecting this. That is one of a hundred thoughts, none of them positive, I have as I drive home to tell Becky.

"Becky, I met with my dermatologist. It wasn't a cyst, I have angiosarcoma, a rare form of cancer."

Becky is stunned and I want so badly to tell her everything will be all right, but I honestly don't know, so I just embrace her.

"We need to tell the kids, Jeff. Can we please call them tonight."

Not one to procrastinate, Becky is right, even though I am still processing the news and have no idea what I will say to them.

We call each child and try to be calm and reassuring.

Sadly, I don't have a corporate emergency protocol to follow for this one. Their silence during each call tells me I am not being very comforting. *Maybe I should have better prepared before springing the news on them,* I think.

A second lab provides their analysis at the request of my newly referred oncologist, Dr. Martinez, who interned at the well-known MD Anderson Cancer Center in Houston, Texas. The lab confirms the original diagnosis; it is angiosarcoma.

Dr. Martinez orders an MRI and CT scan to determine if the cancer is spreading. Fortunately, the images show the cancer is localized, but the tumor I ignored for nine months is now at stage three, based upon its size, depth, and proximity to my skull.

I should reach out to MD Anderson in Houston directly for a second opinion. Over the next few days, I make calls to MD Anderson, but they seem bureaucratic and impersonal, leaving me not totally sold on going all the way to Houston for treatment.

I am able to handle all the doctor's visits and consultations quietly and without raising suspicions at the plant. I figure it's best not to tell my management staff until I know the next steps for treatment. I tell only a very select group of people back at our corporate headquarters.

Dr. Martinez confirms this tumor will require surgery, and he refers to me to a cancer surgeon also practicing in Monterrey. Dr. Santana did his residency at Hope Hospital in Los Angeles,

California. Like MD Anderson, Hope is recognized as one of the finest cancer centers in the United States, so I am feeling comfortable going into my first appointment with Becky by my side.

Dr. Santana carefully explains the procedure to us: "My surgical team and I will excise the tumor and the surrounding tissue all the way to your skull. We will remove all the tissue in an area that is approximately three to four times the diameter of the tumor. The plastic surgeon will close the excision if the post-surgery biopsy shows no sign of cancer. This will probably require grafting skin removed from either your back or your leg."

The good news is, Dr. Santana will perform the surgery at a state-of-the-art hospital just a block from where we live in San Pedro Garza García. And even better news, I will be able to return to work just a few days after the surgery, providing everything goes well, and I do not require follow-up radiation.

Now it is time to tell my staff, so I gather them all in our large conference room. *Don't hold back, Jeff,* I tell myself. *Just get it out there.*

"I have a rare form of cancer," I declare, trying to stay clinical and non-emotional as I describe the surgery and follow-up steps.

The room becomes silent, as if I had told them they were all fired. As I look at their stunned faces, I struggle desperately to hold back my tears. I had been stoic about the whole ordeal up until now. I hadn't truly thought how people other than my immediate family would respond to the news.

"Jeff, I will stay with Becky during the surgery. She will need comforting," says Luci, my amazing HR manager.

"Thank you, Luci, we both appreciate that very much."

Luci has become a good friend, to both Becky and me. One of our first hires, she was so critical in staffing our plant with the best talent. She is one of the managers who arrives at the plant before daylight. Her first words are always "*Hola*, Jeff," followed up with a hug. Luci's "Don't worry, we've got this" attitude is an anchor on days that begin to drift in the wrong direction.

"We can handle the plant, *jefe*, while you recover," the managers all say in unison, like it was rehearsed. But one voice stands out from the others: Sergio's, my assistant plant manager.

More than just a colleague, Sergio is a special friend. He truly is my ear to the ground when it comes to all the personnel required to effectively run this enormous plant. He senses how the crews are handling the pressure of a start-up, and he is quick to tell me when my directives are confusing. I'm especially grateful for the many, many times he brings clarity to a struggling gringo's words during our plant meetings.

"Thank you all very much for your words of encouragement. Your positive voices and strong sense of teamwork, once again, confirm why you are the right leaders for this plant. Now get back to work!" I growl. It's an abrupt phrase I often close meetings with and always with a stern look that turns quickly into a smile.

✤ ✤ ✤

How do I feel with all this cancer stuff going on? Very mixed!

A part of me is scared Jeff is going to die at any time. *How will I cope without him? He's everything to me!*

Another stronger part of me somehow knows, just knows it's going to be okay. Stoic Jeff helps me not get hysterical. I feel the same way I did when my sister was diagnosed with leukemia. At first, I felt devastated that I might lose her, but then God led me to trust it would all be okay.

It's all up to Him, anyway, isn't it? My faith in God has helped me through many a rough time: both my parents' deaths, kids growing up and leaving the nest, staying sober.

✦ ✦ ✦

Just before the surgery, Becky and I have one more consultation with Dr. Santana. "I have good news for you both," he said. "I sent the biopsy to a lab in the United States and the tumor is benign, it is not angiosarcoma. The cell markers for this type of tumor can easily be misinterpreted as cancer, so I felt compelled to have one more laboratory analyze the slides. It is, however, rapidly growing and needs to be removed, using the same surgical procedure, before it causes serious harm.

"Jeff, you can go back to work in two or three days," he adds, "providing there is no infection."

"Super, let's get this over with."

"Once removed, I will, however, send the tumor and surrounding tissue out to the lab to confirm it is benign and that the margins are cancer-free before Dr. Lopez closes up the excision."

✦ ✦ ✦

I wait in the hospital waiting area, pacing and fidgeting not knowing what they would find once they cut into his scalp. When I'm finally able to see him, he has a large bandage on the side of his head with a tube protruding out of it that is pumping oxygen to the open wound. They have to leave it open until the lab can test the margins and be certain it is not cancer.

✤ ✤ ✤

"Holy cow, Jeff! It looks like you were hit by a cannon ball," announces Becky to the entire hospital ward, as Dr. Santana removes the surgical bandage, revealing the open space where the tumor was removed.

Mirrors are placed behind and in front of me so I can see the damage. "Wow, you are not exaggerating, Bec," I confirm.

"Take lots of photos, Becky. The kids will love this."

✤ ✤ ✤

Playing nurse and changing his dressing every day makes me feel so sad Jeff is going through this experience.

Shoot, I feel sad that I am going through it too, I think. *Never, ever, could I imagine one of us would get cancer. We look so healthy. Wasn't God watching over us?*

The next week we meet with the plastic surgeon, Dr. Lopez.

"You'll be surprised what I can do with these magic hands," the doctor says with a big smile on his face.

"Please tell us," Jeff and I encourage.

"You see this loose skin on your neck?" he continues. "I bet you didn't think it would come in handy. I will close this hole by cutting and stretching the loose skin and the skin on Jeff's scalp over the hole and bring it back together from all these different angles and then stitch it closed." He draws a figure of what it would look like after he does all these things, and we can't believe it can be done.

The lab report finally comes back. The margins show no signs of cancer, so Dr. Lopez goes to work. Another surgery is booked, and again I spend time waiting in the hospital.

When Jeff comes out of surgery, he looks like Frankenstein! First his head is shaved bald, of course, the stitching across his scalp is in the shape of a large *Z*. There is no sign of the large hole that had been there.

"I look like Edward Zipperhead," Jeff says as he views the results of his plastic surgery, propped up in his hospital bed.

A ball cap will be a part of his daily wardrobe until his hair grows back and covers the scars.

✣ ✣ ✣

Just two days after the plastic surgery, Becky and I receive a phone call. My mother is in the hospital and her organs are failing.

"Dr. L, can you clear me to travel with Becky to Pennsylvania?" I ask.

"Yes, just make certain to change the bandages every day."

Mom's declining physical condition has slowly progressed since my father's death four years ago. After taking her back to Pennsylvania when the Colorado experiment failed, Becky and I arranged professional care and assistance at home during the daytime to make life easier and more comfortable for Mom.

Her body is frail, but her mind has always remained strong. Amazingly, Mom's memory and mental alertness rival someone less than half her age. Standing less than five feet tall, Pat was still allowed to enlist in the Navy during WWII. Naval Intelligence must have required her talent for memorizing numbers more than they needed her height.

At gatherings with her friends, they would place her in a cozy chair, usually in the center of the event, and Pat would "hold court" as everyone affectionately called it.

Today, however, the attending physician is worried about how I might perceive Mom's condition. "Jeff, I'm concerned you might believe she can recover given her cognitive state, her mental sharpness, but unfortunately that will not happen. Her organs are failing rapidly, and we can only keep her alive through artificial means."

"Dr. Herman, my mother's directive has always been not to use any machines to keep her alive."

"Understood, Jeff, and we will keep your mother as comfortable as possible during her final hours."

✤ ✤ ✤

Mom is lying very still, heavily sedated to relieve her pain, as we arrive at the hospital room. A nurse and her home caregiver are there to greet us.

Becky and I hold her hands and say, "We love you and pray you are at peace."

Shortly afterward, Becky looks at me, and says, "I don't believe she is breathing."

Pat's spirit is now with her daughter, her loving husband, and God.

It is a beautiful memorial service at the church Mom and Dad attended for much of their retired lives. Close family members and many of my parents' friends are in attendance. After the service Mom's ashes are placed in the church's Columbaria next to my father's and sister's ashes.

The church, especially the Columbaria, has long been a special place for both my parents. Brook and Bryce are now seeing the Columbaria Room for the first time. The colorful stained-glass windows and white communion table trimmed in gold were designed, hand-crafted, and assembled by my father, Roy. They make the room warm and inviting.

"Wow, Grandpa Roy was an amazing artist," Brook exclaims.

"He sure was," I say. "He passed that talent along to Aunt Lynne but not your dad. I was probably outside playing baseball with my buds the day Grandpa wanted to endow me with his art skills."

The following day the kids are on a plane back to Texas, and the task of sorting through the items in the house begins.

"Becky, I know it's only been a few days, but I need to get back to Mexico."

"Don't worry, Jeff, I've got this."

So, Becky becomes the executor and graciously handles all the details of my mother's estate. One to never procrastinate about anything, within days, Becky has the house empty and on the market. She is amazing and her selfless work frees me to refocus on the Monterrey plant.

✛ ✛ ✛

Whew! The tumor is benign.

However, Jeff's mom's passing has left a big hole in my heart. I focus instead on getting her estate in order: meeting with the lawyer, meeting with the real estate agent to put her house on the market, divvying up her furniture among family and friends and donating the rest, filing tax returns, notifying the banks of her passing and closing bank accounts, and on and on. It was a big job, but I was up for it.

Finally, all the trauma of the past month is over. We make it to the aftercare appointment with the oncologist, which we had postponed numerous times because of Jeff's focus on the plant start-up. The doctor tells us the scars have healed well and there is no need for another follow-up.

On our way out of his office, I stop and say to Jeff, "Why don't you have the doctor look at the little bump on the crown of your head that you showed me the other night?"

The doctor looks at it.

"It's probably nothing, because it has no color."

"Please biopsy it, anyway," I request firmly.

You never know. At this point, it is better to be safe than sorry.

✢ ✢ ✢

Bad news comes in threes, so the saying goes. First, there was my benign tumor surgery. Second my mom passed, and *numero tres,* melanoma. Just four months after the first surgery, I am back under the knife. It is *Edward Zipperhead Returns,* the sequel!

The excision of the stage three melanoma tumor is the exact surgery I had undergone in the spring except the surgeon also removes two sentinel lymph nodes in my neck to determine if the cancer is spreading. My surgical team is the same, including Dr. Lopez.

After slicing a roadway of S-turns, stretching all the pliable skin he can find and then stitching it all up, Dr. Lopez is still left with a hole to fill, which he plugs with silver laced gauze. Now, it is up to my body, using the surrounding tissue and skin to naturally fill in this sand wedge–sized "divot."

When I wake up from surgery Becky is by my side along with, to my surprise, a longtime friend from my many years working in Mexico.

"Diego! So, good to see you, my friend. Sorry, my throat is hoarse. This time it is not from one of the four-alarm peppers plucked from your garden," I tell him in a barely audible whisper.

"Not to worry, *amigo*. I heard from many of our common friends you were having cancer surgery today, and I just wanted to be here for you and your beautiful wife."

"*Gracias, mi amigo*. Your presence lifts my spirits every time I see you."

Diego, and so many others I have come to call friends, are the biggest reason Mexico is and always will be a very special place for me. Eating the world's best fish tacos while gazing out at the majestic Pacific Ocean off the Baja comes in at a close second.

The post-surgery biopsies come back clean, and now I need to be examined for any visible signs of the melanoma returning only every three months.

My first follow-up exam is all great news. There are no signs of melanoma on my head, or on the rest of my body.

✛ ✛ ✛

In February 2017, we say *adios* to our many friends and my colleagues in Monterrey and return to our mountain home in

Colorado for a new assignment at my company's North American division headquarters just outside of Denver.

It's now April and time for my next skin exam. The appointment is with a dermatologist associated with Colorado University Health organization in Boulder, and she detects several irregular shaped moles on my scalp. Punch biopsies are taken for two moles. In addition, the doctor removes two swollen lymph nodes in my neck to be examined by their lab.

I stand corrected, bad news comes in fours. All my biopsies are positive for melanoma, and I am then referred to Dr. Lang at CU Health's Anschutz Cancer Pavilion in Aurora, Colorado.

Dr. Lang specializes in melanoma treatments. He orders an MRI of my head, neck, and torso. Becky is with me when Dr. Lang says in his direct manner, "You have metastatic melanoma. We have detected ten tumors. Five in your scalp, four in the lymph nodes on the right side of your neck, and there appears to also be one in your back."

My first thought is, *oh great, ten cannon ball size holes on my head, my neck, and my back.* But Dr. Lang chooses a different path of treatment, immunotherapy, a relatively new form of cancer treatment in 2017. Immunotherapy, simply put, uses a combination of therapy drugs to kick my immune system into hyper overdrive in an aggressive effort to destroy the cancerous cells. If it works, I will be able to avoid surgery, at least initially.

"Jeff, once every three weeks you will receive two infusions consisting of two immunotherapy drugs. Initially, you will have four treatment sessions. My staff and I will closely monitor your blood work over the next twelve weeks since there is the potential for side effects that might impact the normal function of key organs."

SHE SAID, HE SAID

"Thank you, doctor. Can I continue to work?"

"Yes, and one more thing. I am going to caution you right up front. Do not google anything about your type of cancer or your treatment. I'll give you all the literature you will need to better understand your cancer and what you can expect during your treatments."

Being the good patient I am, I immediately google "immuno-therapy" and "metastatic melanoma." What stands out the most is the survival rate is fifty-fifty to make it to the five-year mark.

I'm not angry or depressed. I am more like, "Okay, let's get this started!"

I learned years ago from a very insightful speaker to tell myself *what's the worst thing that can happen* and then work through all the scenarios in my mind. The ultimate conclusion: you die and go to heaven. My eternal resting place, heaven, has already been bought and paid for by my Lord and Savior, Jesus Christ.

I don't want to go there just yet, but it will be a damn good plan B, or A, from God's perspective, I suppose.

I do feel sad at times knowing I could be leaving behind, for now, the woman and the family I love with every fiber of my being. What I refuse to do is let myself obsess over it. I believe in the power of prayer, and in giving thanks to the Lord in ALL circumstances. If it's God's will, I'll beat the odds, or I'll go to heaven. Either way, it's a win-win.

✛ ✛ ✛

As we journey through Jeff's newest cancer diagnosis and the immunotherapy treatments, I again experience fear of Jeff leaving me on this earth alone. But also, I again have absolute trust in the Lord that everything will be fine.

I go to the hospital with Jeff for the first treatment, but he goes to the rest alone. They last only about two hours, and he's able to drive home afterward. Jeff is so strong! He insists on going to treatments alone; I guess he doesn't want to be a burden.

The treatments are going well, so we plan a vacation to Costa Rica to see Jake who is working with monkeys in the jungle (he graduated cum laude in Wild Animal Biology from CSU). Then we decide to go over to Cali, Columbia, for our good friends' wedding.

It turns out Jake must leave the country for three days to renew his visa, so we change plans and go to Nicaragua first. I rent a beautiful, large house with a swimming pool that is relatively close to a beach. While we're there, Jeff develops stiffness in his joints and a terrible case of hiccups that won't stop. He can't eat and becomes very weak. Against better judgment, we still go to Cali. We stay at a lovely old hotel, but Jeff immediately goes to bed, where he stays the entire time. He misses the wedding and beautiful reception that followed.

✣ ✣ ✣

Almost immediately upon arriving in Central America I begin to experience side effects from my third immunotherapy session. I develop a rash on my upper body, my arms, and my legs. My skin feels like I'm under assault from a legion of mosquitos. The bumps, the itching, the scratching never cease. My ankles and knees begin to swell, walking is stiff and awkward—even standing is becoming a challenge. I can't keep anything in my system and feel weaker by the day.

I try to ignore it all and not ruin everyone's vacation while we are in Nicaragua. By the time we arrive in Cali, Columbia, it becomes a losing effort and I'm bedridden in our resort accommodations while everyone else is celebrating our friends' wedding and all the festivities surrounding it.

Something is seriously wrong with my body. After years of traveling, I know it's not just the local water. Leaving Cali and flying back to Colorado can't come fast enough. The day after the wedding we have a plane reservation to go back to the States. (Jake and his girlfriend travel on to the Amazon.) I don't know how Becky managed to help me get up, get dressed, and in the cab.

"Becky, would you please pay the cab driver, while I lift the luggage up off the departure curb."

It's a struggle, but I manage to do it, leaving the last ounces of my strength at the revolving door as we slowly walk toward the United ticket counter.

Boom! I collapse to the floor and am in total darkness.

✛ ✛ ✛

We are in line waiting to check our luggage. I turn around as I hear a sound behind me.

"Jeff, what the heck!"

Jeff is on the floor, passed out. It terrifies me and my legs start to buckle.

"Oh, lady, let me help you," a woman says, rushing toward us out of nowhere. She takes off Jeff's shoes and starts rubbing his feet.

Another woman comes up, again out of nowhere, kneels next to Jeff, takes his hand and starts praying over him.

Please don't let him die. Please don't let him die. I'm praying so hard.

Finally, a doctor shows up. Jeff wakes up slowly, and the doctor examines him as best he can.

"I think you're okay, Mr. Jeff. You can travel home but you must agree to stay in a wheelchair the whole time," the doctor orders.

"No worries, doctor. I will make sure he does."

Jeff was too weak to assist me with any of our carry-on. He needed help getting off the plane at our overnight layover in Orlando, and without the generous support of our cab driver, the airport luggage handler, and several loving strangers we would never have made it to our hotel room.

Once in our room, it was too late to order room service or have a local restaurant meal delivered, so dinner was Nab crackers and Diet Coke. Honestly, I don't believe Jeff could have kept anything heavier in his system, so it was probably for the best.

After two very long, horrible, tortuous days, we finally arrive back in Denver.

Jeff had scheduled his fourth treatment for the day after we arrived, but I decide he cannot wait another day. We take the shuttle to our car, and I drive directly from Denver International Airport to the CU Anschutz Hospital.

The emergency room doctor examines Jeff, runs blood tests, and contacts Dr. Lang. Jeff and I are told by the ER doctor that he is severely dehydrated and suffering from auto immune disorder. Jeff's immune system is not just attacking his cancer cells but also his healthy ones. They admit Jeff to the hospital for treatment.

I am so grateful we went directly to the hospital.

✤ ✤ ✤

Becky is insistent that we head straight to the hospital, as we land back in Denver.

"I won't fight you on this, Bec, there's no fight left in me.".

Thank goodness it's practically a straight shot from the Denver International Airport to CU Health-Anschutz Cancer Pavilion in Aurora, Colorado.

It is the Fourth of July, but the hospital is still well staffed to handle my emergency. The blood test results indicate the immunotherapy treatments are attacking my good cells, not just the bad ones, so the ER doctor admits me to a private room on the top floor, overlooking the skyline of Denver. The nurses connect me to a drip bag of electrolytes and inject me with a mega dose of prednisone.

No additional foot rubs from a concerned airport bystander required as life begins to quickly return to my body.

A night of watching magnificent firework displays over the Denver metropolitan skyline and a restful sleep have me starting to feel like myself again. The joint stiffness is rapidly fading. I have an appetite, and even more important, I can drink coffee. Praise God for rich, dark-roast coffee and prednisone.

What doesn't go away is my damn rash that makes me feel like I have taken up residence in a bed of poison ivy.

Dr. Lang reviews my latest labs and says, to our complete surprise, "I know this has not been pleasant, but I believe, after just three treatments, the immunotherapy drugs are working. Let's schedule a CT scan with contrast to determine if the cancer is still present."

The scan shows no signs of cancer in my head, neck, or back.

"Praise God, and thank you very much, Dr. Lang."

The immunotherapy treatments, however, have damaged my thyroid and adrenal glands. Dr. Lang tells me that I'll likely be on medication for the rest of my life. "I'll refer you to an endocrinologist here at Anschutz," he tells me, "who can help you manage both."

"A small price to pay, to be cancer-free. Thank you, doc, but can we get rid of this god-awful rash?"

"Ha, you are welcome, and we'll just keep working on that annoying side effect."

✢ ✢ ✢

By the end of the summer, through the process of elimination, the good doctor finally prescribes an ointment that clears up my rash. It costs as much as my annual Starbucks budget, but oh, is it so worth it.

✢ ✢ ✢

I hit the five-year milestone, and still no signs of the melanoma returning. Then, the sixth year and the seventh year and no signs.

Now, with each passing year, I stand a better chance that some other disease will take my life—either way I die and go to heaven.

Reflections on our Story

BECKY

You never know what life will throw at you. At our wedding, we vowed to stick with each other "in sickness and in health," and we have experienced alcoholism and cancer. God granted us resilience, love for one another through the diseases, and blessings on the other side. God never let go of my hand. Give your fears to God, always trust in Him, whatever the challenge.

JEFF

I am truly grateful no one in a long, flowing robe escorted me down a bright, white tunnel toward eternal rest after I collapsed in Cali airport. And when the day comes that I am greeted at the pearly gates by St. Pete, I'm pretty darn certain he won't offer to rub my ugly feet.

I love this quote from the Christian writer Corrie ten Boom: *"Worry does not empty tomorrow of its sorrow. It empties today of its strength."* Corrie survived the Nazi occupation of her homeland, the Netherlands. It's hard to imagine her life under such a repressive regime, especially after she was caught giving aid to Jews in her community.

Jesus says, "In this world you will have trouble. But take heart! I have overcome the world" (John 16:33). Worry, both of us genuinely believe, will cripple today and blur tomorrow without faith in the One who has overcome this world. When Becky and I remember to walk in faith with God, we experience His comfort, His strength, and we receive genuine hope for a better tomorrow.

The same week I was diagnosed with metastatic melanoma, my very close friend, John, passed away from stomach cancer. I flew down to The Woodlands, Texas, from Colorado, for the celebration of John's life at the same church our families attended together. My son, Bryce, met me at the service, and afterward we went to lunch. I told Bryce my cancer had returned with a vengeance. It was painful to see his reaction as I described the treatments I'd be undergoing over the next several months.

Cancer impacts colleagues, family, and close friends in so many ways, and I do not have the absolute answer for coping with such a devastating disease, but I firmly believe the peace, the calmness, and the assurances that only come from God enabled Becky, and our family, to maintain their hope throughout my cancer treatments.

Sure, I thought about dying and the sadness my family would face, yet, as quickly as those thoughts appeared, I was able to shake them off and visualize life being even better than before my diagnosis. It was important for me to stay positive and focus on being here with Becky and my family, but at times my thoughts would drift beyond this life and toward my heavenly family and what that might be like.

Why did God spare me from death this go around and not my friend? I don't know. What I do know is God is good. His truths, His promises do not change, and because they don't, John is with Him in paradise, where sickness, sorrow, and pain will never be experienced again.

Maybe, I'm still here today, and not in heaven, simply because Jesus and the Holy Spirit wanted me to share this eternal truth with you.

Questions for Discussion

Expand on the great adversities you've had to face in life.

_____

_____

_____

_____

What role has God had in these adversities?

_____

_____

_____

_____

What role did your family and friends have in those difficult times?

_____

_____

_____

_____

How have your adversities played out in your life? What did you learn about yourself and God as you came through them?

_____

_____

_____

_____

CHAPTER 6

RETIREMENT—REMIND ME WHAT DAY THIS IS?

S ometimes on our walks around the hills of our neighbor-hood in Evergreen, we would talk about what to do or where to go when Jeff retired. I retired from being a CPA in 2018 (happily and completely, as in no going back), and Jeff was set to retire in 2019, which then became 2020, which then became 2021. The big guys at his company kept asking him to stay "one more year." Jeff was a great employee, and everyone loved him!

During one walk, Jeff mentions, "I would be willing to dis-cuss moving back to Texas if that is something you are interested in. I can tell you've gotten closer to your sisters back in Texas since your mom passed away."

"Man, that would be awesome," I tell Jeff. "Let me put some thought into it. It is difficult for someone from Texas to lose their Texan identity." (I was born and raised in Dallas.)

Jeff laughs. "We've lived in Colorado for sixteen years. It's been great, and thank you, but I'd say you've paid your dues."

So, after a couple of weeks of thinking and dreaming, I ask Jeff, "Did you really mean what you said about moving back to Texas?"

"Yeah, sure did."

"What do you think about moving to Austin?"

Austin is a place where all Texans want to live. The city has a cool vibe, three beautiful lakes, and is in the middle of the state's rolling Hill Country.

"I love it," he responds. "But it must be in the hills. I need some semblance of mountains."

Then Covid hits! No one who lived through Covid will ever forget wearing a mask, staying home, working from home, and being short of toilet paper. Jeff starts working in his upstairs office behind a closed door all day. And I have a mission: find a house for us in the hills near Austin, Texas. I call a realtor friend from The Woodlands, and she refers me to a realtor in Lakeway, on Lake Travis, just on the outskirts of Austin.

Jeff says that I don't procrastinate, and it's true. I make appointments with Amber and jump on a flight to Austin. She shows me lots of beautiful homes, but every time I find a house I like, poof! It is under contract. Finally, over lunch Amber's phone buzzes.

"Hello. Uh-huh. Uh-huh. Yeah, I'll tell her. Thank you, bye." Amber hangs up and looks at me. "There is a new house that just came on the market. It appears to check all your boxes. I suggest we go see it this afternoon."

"Great. Sure. What time?"

At five that afternoon I call Jeff. "Hi, honey. I'm looking at our new house. It has a beautiful pool (box one), and the kitchen has a double oven (box two). The house is built with white Austin stone (box three) and has an open floor plan (box four) with the master bedroom down on the first floor (box five). I'll send you some videos."

"Looks awesome, Bec. I love the pool. Do you want to make an offer?"

"I think I better make an offer soon. These houses are going quickly."

I had the house under contract by eight that evening.

✣ ✣ ✣

I look forward to hearing more about the house when Becky calls tonight. Meanwhile, I try to stay focused on work but looking out the window of my work-from-home office all I see is Bergen Peak and the rolling green meadow below its mountain pines and aspens. *I should turn my desk around to avoid this distracting view. Window blinds were invented to keep you focused on work, so close them, Jeff.*

This isolation nonsense from the Covid outbreak is making me wish I didn't have five more months to go before I retire. Suddenly, the phone rings; it's my boss, Stan.

"Jeff, what are your plans next year?" he asks, always straight to the point.

"Stan, you know I'm retiring in January, and as we speak, Becky is in Austin, Texas, looking for our retirement home."

"Austin. I love Austin! Would you stay on with the company for another year if I let you work from your new home in Texas?"

Stan is a great boss. His enthusiasm is infectious. He has the ability to motivate people in a way that makes them want to grab a sword and go slay a dragon—including this sixty-seven-year-old guy. Simply put, it's very hard to say no to Stan.

"Yes, but January 2022 is it, final, done, complete, over!"

Later in the evening, Becky calls to tell me the house is under contract. Mission accomplished! The home checks all the boxes. It wasn't built at seven thousand five hundred feet above sea level, just seven hundred fifty feet, but it's still high enough to see for miles in all directions and is perfect for viewing Texas Hill Country orange sunrises and sunsets that stretch across an endless horizon.

✤ ✤ ✤

Back in Colorado, we put our house in Evergreen on the market, and it sold rather quickly. We donated a lot of furniture, clothes, and knick-knacks and gave even more to 1-800-GOT-JUNK?. We thought we were downsizing when we moved to Colorado (ha-ha joke's on us). After the closing, off we go to Austin. It is a long drive. We spend the first night sleeping on pool lounger cushions in the master bedroom. The movers will arrive the next day. Yes, we did all of this during Covid.

Jeff finds an upstairs bedroom in our new home to set up his remote office. He spends all day on the phone and Zoom calls and doesn't come out until dinner, except for coffee and a protein bar. On October 15, 2021, he finally retires and shuts that office door for good. We never looked back.

✤ ✤ ✤

We arrived in Texas, at our new hacienda, the first day of September, just six weeks after Becky began her search. Did I mention Becky does not procrastinate?

A very hot, late summer afternoon temperature in the mountains of Colorado is, at its worst, in the low eighties. That's the low temperature of the day here in the Texas Hill Country, and by mid-afternoon, when I step outside, I'm smacked by nearly triple digit temps. *This is going to take some getting used to for sure. Can't wait to see that first utility bill.*

In all fairness to Hill Country natives, they seldom complain about the heat, and I'm convinced that's because they've visited their cousins enough in Houston, where the humidity levels match the ninety-five-degree temperatures every stinking day in the summer, and then it's even muggier at night.

✣ ✣ ✣

We are quickly settling into our new home and getting to know the neighbors through the Friday evening cul-de-sac parties. Covid masks are always optional, according to our newfound block partiers.

Okay, curious minds need to know, so I break into a friendly conversation with the guys and ask, "How come no masks?"

"We live just far enough outside of the recently defunded police state of Austin to make our own life choices," the cul-de-sac host answers in a defiant voice. The explanation is unanimously confirmed with a "yup" and a toast from all my fellow partiers.

✣ ✣ ✣

Working from home is becoming more and more of a grind, rather than a convenient, safe space from Covid. What could have been solved in the office breakroom while grabbing a cup of coffee with a coworker now requires a Zoom call, and there are plenty of those every day.

I love it when I get to travel to our plants, even though I must mask-up, carry sanitary hand gel, and record my temperature before entering the building. Nothing beats interacting with real people in real physical surroundings. I feel isolated way too much working from home, and the frustration builds as I try to help solve each day's complex problems through the tiny camera lens on my computer screen. *Enough is enough, I'm giving notice. My final day will be October fifteenth. That's three months, plenty of notice.*

There are other reasons, too, if I am honest. I just celebrated my fourth year of being cancer-free, and I want to enjoy more time with Becky and our family, as I head toward that critical five-year milestone. And there's also the siren's call of tennis. Tennis is the game I love, and my mythological mistress has been ignored for far too many years.

October arrives and it is time to fly back to Colorado to complete my retirement papers. After eighteen months of working remotely, I just want to go back to our headquarters, sign my retirement papers, have a cup of Starbucks coffee with my administrative assistant, Joyce, and then hike the mountains with Becky.

But Joyce digs her heels in. "Coffee won't work," she says. "We at least need to have a luncheon."

So, Joyce, being the best of the best, especially when it comes to organizing events, reserves a banquet room at a local hangout and emailed invitations.

I'm going to miss Joyce a lot, along with her admin sidekick, Corina. When we were working in person and I'd be there hours past quitting time, they would stick their heads into my office, frown at me, and say, "Don't be a dope!"

"Yeah, you are both right. I need to wrap up this day and get home to Becky, but hey, isn't that the pot calling the kettle black?"

Funny, all those years working together, we never stopped being dopes.

Okay, lunch is over, time for a speech. Just make it from the heart.

"Thank you for an amazing career. I owe so much to you, Becky, for your support and encouragement. Thank you for being there, always. And a huge thanks to everyone here, you always strived for excellence and that motivated me to do the same. I will miss y'all."

Instead of being overwhelmed with sadness, as my long career with one company was coming to an end, I feel joy, contentment, and peace. It really is time to say farewell, and I am totally good with it. Now, it's off to the mountains to hike with my best friend before heading back to Texas.

✢ ✢ ✢

I love our house in Austin. It has a Mediterranean vibe. The flooring is tiled (Jeff's favorite) throughout the main level, and the kitchen is large and white. We have balconies to watch the beautiful Hill Country sunsets while we sit in our oversized wicker chairs enjoying a cool evening breeze. And of course, it has the mandatory backyard swimming pool.

I start my life in Austin with Pilates in the morning, afternoons lying next to and in the pool, and some tennis thrown in occasionally. But while Jeff is still holed up in his office working or traveling for work, I find I need something more in my life. They say to follow your passion, and I have always been passionate about clothes. So, I researched how to start an online clothing business and end up meeting a woman through Facebook who had started one with her daughter.

"Please tell me how you started your online clothing shop," I plead.

"Well, first you must register a name for your store with the Secretary of State and get a business license and sales tax number," I'm told. *Ugh, not taxes again.* "Set up a Shopify store; it's very easy. And then post pictures of your clothing and prices. We buy our clothing from online wholesalers and drop-ship our orders."

No online wholesalers for me. I am going to Dallas to buy clothes from Apparel Mart, a landmark in the city. Oh, I can't wait. I've wanted this my whole life.

She tells me some more details, and I thank her profusely before hanging up the phone. It doesn't take me long (maybe a couple of days, ha-ha) to set up my clothing store. I come up with the name Apple's Closet (in honor of Brook), register with the Texas AG office, and get a tax ID. When setting up an account with Shopify, I find the name Apple's Closet is taken. So, I draft a DBA (doing business as) and use the legal name Apple's Tree Clothing Company.

Now comes the fun stuff, buying the clothes I will sell. I called my youngest, Jack. He lives in Brooklyn and works for an upscale clothing line in Soho. (Jack has been in fashion since he was a teenager.)

"Jack, how would you like to meet me in Dallas and pick out some clothing for my new online store? I've named it Apple's Tree Clothing Company."

"What are you up to now, Mom?"

"Oh, I got a bee in my bonnet and decided to start an online clothing store. I'll need to go to the Apparel Mart in Dallas to pick out the clothes I want to sell. I thought it would be fun to do it together." So, I fly Jack to Austin, and we fly together to Dallas, go to the market at Apparel Mart, and buy some clothes. Looking back, we should have focused on the less expensive Temp Exhibitors, but we went up to the designers' showrooms where the buyers get individual attention. We make appointments and show up for our own personal fashion show. We are in heaven. Being new to the business, I don't focus on prices. I am not really in it to make big bucks; I want to have fun working with my son. Being an accountant, I should have known that was a big mistake!

On Christmas, Bryce and his wife give us a large white backdrop for photo shoots of the clothes I list on Shopify. I convince my friends, all beautiful, to be my models. A friend from church takes the pictures, and we have a good time doing the photoshoots.

I never sell one thing online. Instead, I host fashion shows, mini markets at ladies' homes, markets at county fairs, and just have friends over to shop. I sell the most at fashion shows and parties at my house. I need time to figure out the best strategy for ordering clothes so I don't end up with so many left over at the end of the season. Obviously, winging it isn't working. But I don't have time because this venture is eating me up financially. I end up selling as much inventory as I could to friends at cost and donate the rest to a charity for financially challenged women. We are sure to get a large tax write-off this year.

So, my business venture is somewhat of a bust, but boy do I have fun doing it. If I do it again, next time I'll pay more attention, be more frugal, and take small steps instead of big leaps.

✢ ✢ ✢

One of the greatest joys of moving to Austin for me was getting connected with Red Rocks Church–Austin. It's a satellite church of the multi-campus, Colorado-based, non-denominational church we had belonged to since 2008.

The original Red Rocks Church started in a dilapidated building on the grounds of a "creepy old theme park" in Golden, Colorado—an affectionate description lead pastor Shawn Johnson often used in his sermons.

Red Rocks Church–Colorado could barely fill the front row seats their first Sunday in January 2005. It wasn't much different for the Austin campus's first service back in early January 2019, from what I hear. But when you walk into Red Rocks for the first time, there's something transforming, a sense of belonging, that you are welcomed just as you are—life's baggage and all. Friends tell their friends. Kids tell their parents. College students tell college students, and before you know it, the pastors are kindly asking members to attend a Saturday night service to make room for first timers to attend on Sunday mornings. You don't just want to belong. You want to serve, to be a part of Jesus's plan for his church.

We drive to RRC–Austin for the first time in October 2020. The church is having a live service for the first time since March, when the Covid outbreak had cities mandating the shutdown of large gatherings.

We are greeted by Ryan Wekenman, one of the three young pastors. Doug Wekenman and Ethan Matott were the other two who planted RRC–Austin. Ryan is wearing a faded, dark blue hooded sweatshirt with RRC ATX printed in bold white letters across the front. "I really love that sweatshirt," Becky says. Without hesitation, Ryan pulls the sweatshirt over his head and hands it to her. Yes, Ryan literally gives Becky the (sweat) shirt off his back.

We quickly find ourselves serving at RRC–Austin, too. We help on the café team where we use Curtis, the giant, steaming, clanging, stainless steel coffee maker that came from the satellite Red Rocks Church that met in the Evergreen High School, where we attended and served after returning from our time in Monterrey, Mexico. Eventually, it became cost prohibitive for Red Rocks Church to continue having services on Sundays at the school, so much of the equipment, along with Curtis and several young, energetic, visionary staff members, made the trek to Texas.

The feeling of community isn't just reserved for Saturday and Sunday services. We also joined a Life Group that meet on Wednesday nights at the home of our group leaders, Carly and Evan. Most of the group are comprised of young couples, either engaged or recently married. Becky and I are the sages in the room, purely based upon age and life experience, certainly not theology. It is fun learning together, sharing life stories, and getting a younger generation's perspective on how they stay anchored to their faith.

Occasionally, we take a break from our Wednesday night routine and gather for a special meal at one of the many amazing restaurants in the Austin area. One of the many talents the young couples possess is selecting the perfect dining establishment. Even something as simple as eating Asian-Mex on picnic tables under the stars make it a night to remember.

✢ ✢ ✢

With Jeff's encouragement I begin taking tennis lessons. We join a tennis club in the neighborhood called World of Tennis, where I also took Pilates. I hadn't touched a tennis racket since living in Monterrey. In addition to lessons, I also sign up for tennis drills and clinics. I meet some other ladies at a tennis camp the club puts on every spring and fall. Then, I met a lovely lady waiting for a Pilates class to begin.

"Your nails are beautiful. Where did you get them done?" I ask.

"Oh, a friend has a nail boutique down on 620. My name is Mary."

"Nice to meet you. My name is Becky. Would you give me the number for the boutique?"

"Sure. It looks like the class is about to start; we had better get in there. I love this instructor, have you had her?"

That was the beginning of a wonderful friendship.

Mary and her friends are my best customers at Apple's Tree. She and I spend a lot of time together lying by our pool, shopping at Lakeway's many boutiques, going out for lunch, and taking walks. It is so much fun having a bunch of girlfriends to hang out with.

After the tennis camp, a few ladies decide to form a team to play in the Women's Team Tennis of Austin league and ask me to join them. We always play doubles tennis. At our first match, I just froze. I have always had team sports anxiety. I have a fear of looking stupid, letting the team down, and doing it wrong. This fear kept me from participating in team sports for many, many years. I had almost forgotten about it, but it comes back with vengeance. Well, we lose our first match without scoring any points. The worst. My partner is furious with me. The next week's match I am even more anxious. This time I play with the team captain. Again, we don't score any points. I am so embarrassed. It is so painful I drop out of the team and go back to playing in the fall tennis camp where I excel. I have become the black sheep of women's tennis at the club. No one wants me on their team. It hurts, but I hold my head up and just play tennis for fun. Then things change.

✦ ✦ ✦

Tennis is foremost on my mind since retiring. I line up private lessons with the head tennis pro, Ava, at the tennis and fitness club. I also jump into as many group drills as I can find, connect with a gang of guys who love to play at six in the morning, join a US Tennis Association team, and play social doubles on Saturday nights with Becky. Tennis life is good.

Yup, I am getting my tennis groove on. Then, one Friday morning in late January 2022, just three months into retirement, that mythological Siren sends me crashing into the rocks.

Ava hits a drop shot where the ball lands close to the net. It was something we had practiced, countlessly, in my weekly lesson. I sprint to the net to hit the ball. Only this time when I plant my right foot to stop my momentum, my foot rolls, and I body slam onto the court and end up motionless on my back.

Ava, in her calm, confident, coaching voice says, "just relax a minute. You'll be fine, then we can start hitting again."

"That sounds good, Ava," I reply. "Only one minor snag; I can't move my leg."

I'd fractured my femur, just below the hip joint, so badly it was hanging by a tread.

Ava grabs her cell phone and calls Becky. "I think Jeff is okay," she calmy says, "but you better come to the club." Next Ava calls the club's first responders.

As I become more consciously aware of what just happened, I also become very much aware of the pain, and it is unbearable. Thankfully, the club responders, the EMT's, and Becky are on the court within minutes.

The EMTs efficiently assess my injury, place me on a special stretcher, load me into the ambulance, and drive me to the trauma center in Austin, with Becky closely following in her car.

✛ ✛ ✛

That fateful morning, I am working around the house when Ava calls. She makes it sound like Jeff has just fallen on the tennis court, so I finish what I am doing, brush my teeth, go to the bathroom, and generally take my time getting to the club. When I turn into the parking lot and see the EMT van and fire truck, I immediately start freaking out. *Uh oh, I should have hurried over.* I go to the court where Jeff is lying motionless on the ground. I lean over him and say, "Hi, honey." I'm not sure if he knows I am even here. The EMTs rush him to a hospital I had never heard of. I had to look it up on my phone. My heart is pounding all the way there. I find Jeff at the emergency wing, and we wait in the hall forever for a room.

✛ ✛ ✛

Dr. Firestone, the on-duty orthopedic surgeon, immediately orders an imaging scan. Afterward he shows us the damage, and it isn't pretty. He schedules surgery for early the following morning. It all happens so fast. I wake up in the recovery room after the surgery with a long titanium rod permanently secured into my femur with Texas-size screws.

That afternoon, Dr. Firestone comes into my room and gives us the good news. "The surgery was successful," he says. "Your repaired leg is load bearing now, so you can get out of bed, and start walking right away. I'll prescribe physical therapy and will see you in a week at my office."

"Thanks, for patching me up so quickly, doc. Will I be able to play tennis again?"

"The short answer is, yes, but much depends on how you embrace your rehab."

"That won't be an issue," I promise him.

I look like a ninety-year-old man as I shuffle through the hospital hallways supported by a walker and my backside embarrassingly peeking out from the hospital gown. Becky encourages me every awkward step of the way. The next day, after one more shuffle of shame, I am discharged from the hospital.

They gave me painkillers before and after my surgery, but I don't become addicted to those. Instead, I develop a heavy dependency on Ava's "crack" cookies, as we call them. It's her special recipe containing chocolate chunks, coconut, butterscotch chips, and lots and lots of sugar and could hold their own on any reality baking show. She frequently and thoughtfully brings them by the house and even takes some to Becky's fashion parties.

Physical therapy is a grind, but by the end of May, I am a second-degree balance board black belt. Walking and running became natural motions again, and by mid-June, I am back hitting tennis balls with Ava on court number three, the scene of the crime.

✜ ✜ ✜

Becky and I are hardly back from a quick, but fun road trip to Southern California in late May when we get the best news possible: we are going to be grandparents! Bryce and his beautiful wife, Brittany, are expecting.

I love to give surprises, but waiting for them is borderline cruel in my book. I need to know the baby's sex, but Bryce and Brittany want to do a reveal in the late fall. How am I to know what sports gear and team clothing to stock up on. Do I get a bucket of baseballs or softballs? What color of Denver Broncos onesie to order? Is Crush orange unisex? Five months is an eternity when you are an expectant grandfather.

✢ ✢ ✢

So exciting! Our first grandbaby. The only problem is Bryce and Brittany live in Tomball (near Houston), and we are in Austin, three hours away. We both think about the situation separately and then discuss it together. We are retired and can live anywhere, like The Woodlands, for example, which is only forty minutes from Tomball. We love Austin and our friends here, but it's a grandbaby, and we want to be a part of his life. We are able to attend the big reveal and all the baby showers. It's a boy. We sell our beautiful Austin home with a swimming pool surprisingly quick, pack up, and take off for The Woodlands.

Brady is born January 28, 2023. What a joy he is in our lives.

We really don't know where in The Woodlands we want to live, so we decide to move into an apartment (gasp!) by Lake Woodlands. It is a lovely high-rise apartment with plenty of room, floor to ceiling windows with views of the water, a nice gym, and a beautiful swimming pool at the edge of the lake. In addition, there is a Pure Barre gym around the corner where I (Becky) can walk to work out.

✛ ✛ ✛

Full circle. We were back where life, as a couple and blended family, began twenty-four years earlier. I (Jeff) know for a fact now that God has a sense of humor. No one more than me criticizes the heat and humidity of Southeast Texas, but God blessing us with Brady makes that heat kinda, sorta bearable. As a matter of self-preservation, I am now a minimalist: shorts and T-shirts for nine months, shorts and sweatshirts for three months.

Heavenly Father, am I (Jeff) allowed one more gripe? Every stinkin' store and restaurant in Southeast Texas has their air conditioning set at sixty degrees. You endure goosebump chills while inside, then walk back outside into the heat and humidity only to be temporarily blinded when your sunglasses fog up. Come on Houstonians, you know I'm right about this. Can I get an amen?

✛ ✛ ✛

We are very lucky that the tennis club we joined in Austin is part of Club Corp which also includes The Woodlands Country Club as a member. This means we are able to transfer our membership for a reduced fee. I start taking lessons and drills like I did in Austin. One day, the tennis pro asks me if I am interested in joining a team (yikes, not again). I smile and say sure (if at first you don't succeed, try and try again). I don't think about it. I just do it. I play with the lovely ladies, and they ask me to join their team. It is a C2 level team, which is the lowest on the totem pole.

It's with older ladies, so it's my cup of tea. I have fun playing tennis and taking drills with the new team all summer, but then league play starts in late August. Oh, boy. Even though I play on line four (the lowest) most of the time, I lose every match. I just freeze out of fear every week before playing. Finally, I say to myself, *enough is enough. I have got to lick this problem, or I'll never enjoy tennis.*

"Honey, I can't seem to beat this anxiety I feel before every tennis match. I want to see a sports psychologist." Yay, he's not laughing.

"Okay. Do you know someone to go to?"

"I'll have to do some research. I hope I can find one in The Woodlands."

Well, the closest sports psychologist I find is in Tomball. It is a thirty-minute trek but worth my time.

"Hi, Becky. My name is Sandra."

"Hi, Sandra. I'm glad I found you."

"Tell me what's bothering you."

"Well, I have severe anxiety whenever I play a tennis match. It's been that way for me with sports ever since I was a kid. I'm not sure, but I think I'm afraid of losing, have a fear of failure."

I precede to tell her about my tennis experience in Austin and how I got "blacklisted."

"That's a terrible experience, Becky. Have you ever heard of a technique called blindspotting? It's worked for a lot of my clients, and I think it will work for you, too."

(In psychology, a blind spot is part of a person's thinking, behavior, or perception that they are unaware of. For me, my blind spots are subconscious and include limitations and shortcomings.)

"Okay," I said. "Let's go for it."

She gets me to talk about my fears from way back when it came to team sports and the stories leading up to my sense of failure. I see her only four or five times, but the fears start evaporating, and I start winning matches! Now I play with more confidence than ever before. Although I don't always win, I don't beat myself up over losing. I just go on to play another day, with maybe a lesson or two thrown in. This is a mini miracle in my life. So much freedom!

Reflections on Our Story

BECKY

Oh, my goodness. Lots of big changes in our lives. For some, this would be too overwhelming, but we took it one step at a time even though we did it in two and a half years. I had to give up a lot of things when we moved. I gave up friends in Colorado when we moved to Austin and friends in Austin when we moved to The Woodlands. I had to give up the mountains first and then the gorgeous Austin sunsets. I had to give up being a mountain girl, but it was worth it to return to my roots as a Texan. It was good to be back to the warm weather (yes, I love the heat and humidity), and a grandson.

JEFF

Nothing in nature has ever given me a sense of wonder like the Rocky Mountains of Colorado, and I would have been perfectly content to retire in those mountains, but nothing in my human experience has awed me like the joyful smile radiating from our first grandchild. And for that reason, there are no second thoughts about leaving Colorado.

We now have two grandchildren, and "Lord willing and the creek don't rise," we will live to experience the joy of even more grandkids.

—————BECKY—————

My biggest regret is quitting the tennis team in Austin. I felt a lot of shame and hurt feelings around it. It's true what parents try to teach their children: "don't quit or you'll become a quitter." I quit a lot of things in this season of my life. But I believe God put the thought of seeing a sports psychologist in my mind after we moved to The Woodlands. This simple act of trust changed my life for the better in so many ways, and not just in tennis. So, trust the process. "All things work together for good to those who love God" (Rom. 8:28 NKJV).

—————JEFF—————

So often we expect our outcomes to rise to the level of our perceived ability. Unfortunately, when it comes to competition, that just ain't so for the average joe, and I would venture to say it holds true for work, family, and life in general.

Patrick Mouratoglou, renowned tennis coach for the greatest female player of my lifetime, Serena Williams, says not to beat yourself up when you fall short of winning, but instead to have the attitude, "Okay, now I know what I need to go work on."

I continually remind myself, even in retirement, that there's something that needs improving in my life. Some

SHE SAID, HE SAID

days it's living out my faith, other days it's my marriage, and most days it's my tennis game.

"Becky? We love Becky!" her old Austin tennis teammates told me when I ran into them by chance one day. Becky falsely believed being liked by her teammates was dependent on her performance. I had similar thoughts early in my career, especially when project execution fell miserably short of plan. When we get down on ourselves, we just need to recognize it's the Evil One coming to "steal and kill and destroy" (John 10:10) our joy and then remind ourselves that God always sees us like Becky's teammates truly saw her.

King David describes us as this incredible person that God knit together in our mother's womb (Psalm 139:13). "Becky? We love Becky!" Expect and receive God's love, without condition.

Questions for Discussion

What steals your joy? How do you overcome it?

_____

_____

_____

_____

Do you find others want to plan events for you, or even worse, your life? How do you tend to react?

_____

_____

_____

_____

Does seeking the approval of others play more of a critical role in your life than it should?

_____

_____

_____

_____

CHAPTER 7

FINANCES, GIVING, AND GIVING BACK

W e have never been ones to ring up a bunch of credit card debt. If we use a credit card to make a purchase, we usually pay it off at the end of the month. It isn't something we sit down and discuss; we both are just opposed to debt. We did have a mortgage on the house in Evergreen and occasionally took out a car loan. It's extremely difficult to raise a family, own a home, and drive cars on a cash basis if you are a regular working joe and jane. We didn't go out to eat much or drink alcohol, two factors alone that helped to keep our expenses in check and manage all the costs associated with raising four children.

Reflecting back, I see how God blessed us so much in this area. Jeff paid for some things, I paid for others, and there was always some left over. We rarely fought over money, except Jeff would occasionally get frustrated with my spending.

Honestly, there was a time when I was pursuing my coaching career that Jeff had to bail me out and then rein me in. I kept thinking, *Just one more course and then I'll be a successful coach.*

But that was a lie the sellers of the courses were feeding me. I needed Jeff's financial wisdom at that point in my life, and he was happy to bestow it on me. As his mother used to say, "He delivers his hints with a sledgehammer."

Also, I can get a little manic about shopping when I'm feeling high on life. Even now sometimes it's hard for me to stop. It's sad, but I need to pray for restraint.

✛ ✛ ✛

I have two addictions in life: Jeeps and coffee. Fortunately, I never let either empty our bank account and leave us worrying how we would make it to the next payday. There were times I would go brain dead and get something practical for the family like a full-sized SUV. Fortunately, I always came to my senses and headed right back to the Jeep dealership. As for java, I like it hot and black. When the barista asks if I want milk or cream, the immediate reply is, "Never!" No fussy coffee drinks for me. This simple act of financial restraint saves me a thousand dollars a year. What better way to justify a brand-new Jeep Rubicon Unlimited Recon Edition with custom wheels and thirty-five-inch tires that never sees a muddy mountain trail, right?

My daughter, Brook, loves Jeeps too. While still in college, she was T-boned in her Hummer H3 by a full-sized SUV that ran a red light. Amazingly, she walked away from her vehicle without a scratch. Even more amazing, the insurance company totaled that eight-year-old Hummer and gave Brook a twenty-thousand-dollar check.

"Wow! That's a nice check, Brook. What car are thinking about buying now?"

"Dad, I really want a soft-top, two-door Jeep."

"Great, let's go to the Jeep dealership and see what they have."

Sure enough, the dealership had a low-mileage, used Wrangler in all black with a lift kit, customs wheels, and oversized knobby tires. Just the Jeep every college-aged girl in Colorado desires.

Then, reality sets in. The dealership's sales rep hands us an offer sheet. Twenty-three thousand dollars, firm. Just three thousand dollars over her budget.

"Dad, I really want that Jeep."

"Brook, here's the perfect opportunity to learn about sticking to a budget. If the dealer really wants to sell it, just wait a few days. If they don't call, my guess is there are a few more black soft-top Jeeps available somewhere in this town."

It was hard not to give Brook the difference so she could drive her dream Jeep home that night, but the lesson in living within your means was more important.

"Tree, guess what," Brook said. "The salesman called me back and said they would sell me the Jeep for twenty thousand."

"Apple, that is fantastic. I'm so proud of you for walking away the other night, and even prouder that you stuck to your budget."

✢ ✢ ✢

During the years we were focused on careers and raising kids, we consistently contributed money to the church, and over time, we learned to use the tithe (10 percent) as our guide. Additionally, we regularly gave to charitable organizations, usually close to where we lived. But later in our lives, especially after Jeff was promoted to a level where he received stock options, we started giving above and beyond. We played this giving game with each other. When God blessed us financially, and even sometimes when He didn't, we would throw out dollar amounts to give above and beyond to the church. I usually started with what I thought was reasonable. Then Jeff would come up with a ridiculously high amount. We would eventually agree on a number somewhere between the middle and the higher figure. Believe me, this was scary for me. I always had a scarcity complex (I don't know why because I never lacked anything financially).

Jeff would always say, "You can't out give God."

We would send the church a check and never feel we lacked in other areas of our finances. God blessed us once again when Jeff retired and we sold our house in Austin, so we really stretched ourselves again with the amount we donated to the church. Once more, we never felt a hole in our bank account. God just kept on blessing us. The joy we felt in our hearts was so much greater than anything that money could have bought.

✦ ✦ ✦

I started out my newfound church life as a skeptic of giving, especially whenever a pastor talked about money and tithing. Most of my cynicism, if I'm being honest, was not from good theology. It came from too many tabloids and made-for-TV movies. Mention giving, and all I pictured were pastors flying around in private jets, wearing custom suits, and their wives with bouffant hairdos and ten-inch eyelashes shedding crocodile tears, as they asked their congregation to give generously.

That is not Red Rocks Church. They say, "You are not giving to a church; you are giving through a church." Something I never heard in my early days as a Christian.

Their nondescript buildings converted to worship halls also made it clear to me the pastors were not concerned with ornate buildings on sprawling campuses or flying to book signings in their private jet. The generosity of those who give through Red Rocks Church has impacted thousands of individuals living in local and worldwide communities, hundreds of men and women incarcerated at state prisons, and many, many other churches. Best of all, God receives all the glory, not someone with ten-inch eyelashes and running mascara.

✢ ✢ ✢

It all began one summer when the boys were staying with their dad.

I was having lunch with my friend Shelly from work.

Kinda out of the blue she says, "Doug and I are volunteering this summer to be part of the work crew for Young Life Camp at Lake Powell. Do you and Jeff want to come too?"

"What's Lake Powell?" I asked.

"It's a huge lake in Arizona and Utah. It's so beautiful. Our family has been going there for years."

"Sounds cool. Jeff and I have been wanting to volunteer for some time now but didn't know how or where. Let me talk to him about it tonight."

Later that evening while cleaning up after dinner, I asked Jeff, "What do you think about joining Shelly and Doug as a work crew volunteer at a Young Life Camp on Lake Powell next June?

Shelly was telling me about it at lunch today, and it sounds like a fun way to volunteer."

"I think that sounds great. What else can you tell me about it?" Jeff said.

"That's all I know. Let's call Shelly right now and tell her we'd love to volunteer."

The camp was organized by Shelly's son and his girlfriend who led the high school's Young Life group. We went to a meeting one evening at the son's apartment and met the other volunteers, who were all super nice.

At four in the morning on a Saturday in June, we piled into cars with the other volunteers and drove eight hours to Lake Powell. Exhausted, we piloted our three well-worn rental house boats (one for the girls, one for the boys, and one for the crew) to a cove selected by the leaders. If you've never been to Lake Powell, you have got to go. It's a big, very deep lake in Arizona and Utah, surrounded by huge natural rock walls that make you think of the Grand Canyon. It's stunning.

At the cove, we anchored and tied up the boats and groomed the beach for meals and play. Jeff and Doug were part of the work crew. My friend and I were in the kitchen. They appointed me to be the nurse, which makes no sense. The week of lake activities and hard work means a lot to me. I had always been nervous to help others, fearing I would do something wrong and upset someone. While there I learned to just jump in and do the next thing without thinking and analyzing. I became a helper to others.

✢ ✢ ✢

I love physical labor and all things mechanical, so being a part of the work crew for the Young Life Lake Powell trip was a good fit for me. "Skipper" Doug and his "Little Buddy" Jeff didn't lack for challenges. We had to fix the boat generators, change the anchoring points every day as the lake's water level changed, unclog toilets, deal with failing fuel pumps, tier and rake the sloped beaches for dining tables and games, fuel the motorized water toys, and pilot the girls' houseboat back to the marina to empty an overflowing waste bilge. Needless to say, this work made for long days and short nights. And would someone please explain to me how twenty teenage girls can possibly fill an enormous waste bilge in less than twenty-four hours?

Star gazing while sleeping on the top deck at night and watching movies projected on an IMAX theater–sized canyon wall were just a couple of the amazing memories I had from that volunteer trip. If you ever houseboat on Lake Powell, those two are essential activities.

On the final day, many of the teenagers were baptized in the shallow water of the cove. Experiencing that event from the top deck of the houseboat and seeing the joyful smiles of each teenager as their bodies emerged from the water made those long days and short nights oh, so worth it.

✦ ✦ ✦

Back in Evergreen, Jeff and I volunteered at Red Rocks Church. Jeff worked in the parking lot while I was taking care of toddlers in Kids Rock. In Austin, we volunteered at the café at Red Rocks Church–Austin. We had a blast doing this. Before and in between services, we helped make the coffee and set up the coffee counter located in the lobby of the church. We had an impressive selection of creamers—every flavor known to mankind. We also welcomed new visitors and chatted with the people who regularly attended services. Our egos were stroked as we kind of became famous. A larger-than-life poster of the two of us in front of the café graced the lobby for several months. We prayed to God to give us humility (ha-ha).

Settling into our new home back in The Woodlands, after our grandson Brady arrived, Jeff looks at me one day and says, "Can we start volunteering? We certainly have the time."

"Sure," I agree. "Where and doing what?"

So, a new activity was added to our calendars. We searched for volunteer opportunities with Interfaith, a nonprofit social service agency for families, children, and seniors in The Woodlands and surrounding areas. We chose to work alternately between the food bank and the thrift store called Hand Me Up. The food bank isn't too exciting, but they need help. What I really enjoy is the thrift store. We have become experts at arranging the donated art on the back wall. I am the decorator, and Jeff is the muscle, moving large paintings around. We also do other jobs: testing electronics, steaming clothes, sifting through clothing donations, and tagging items for the floor. I donate some clothes I don't need anymore. It's a very worthy cause. All the sales proceeds go back to Interfaith and thus the community.

✤ ✤ ✤

Volunteering has always been important to me, and I wanted to find something Becky and I could do together once we retired. Interfaith of The Woodlands is the perfect fit. Volunteering has been pure fun, especially during the holidays. Testing strands of donated Christmas lights, inspecting dozens of inflatable Santas for leaks, or busily assembling donated Christmas trees just to watch them fly off the shelves is truly rewarding.

Confession, if you had asked me to decorate for Christmas at our place, you'd be lucky to see the tree put up by Christmas Eve. I love decorations at Christmas and enjoy seeing homes and local businesses colorfully lit up at night. But in the back of my mind while I help Becky decorate, all I can visualize is breaking down the nine-foot artificial tree, getting angrier by the minute because it doesn't fit perfectly back into the box it came in; placing all the carefully wrapped bulbs in the tubs marked "Xmas" only to forget, once more, to save enough hooks for next year; and taping up the table decorations box, then gazing over at the fireplace mantel and seeing the ceramic Swiss village. Yes, I can overthink what should be a joyful holiday tradition.

Reflections on Our Story

BECKY

It's hard to part with money when there's no immediate tangible benefit. That's why many people don't give. We didn't give much either in the beginning. Then we looked around and saw how much God had blessed us. We decided we needed to share our blessings. I say we decided, but God laid it on our hearts. We never felt a loss, even when we gave a lot. That takes a lot of trust, but it's not hard to trust God.

I had lunch with a friend recently. She said she was afraid to totally retire because she feared not having enough to do.

I asked her, "What about volunteering?" She was stumped.

"I never thought about it."

If this sounds like you, ask God to lead you to ways of giving back. Your heart will feel lighter, your smile will be brighter, and you will feel closer to others after doing so.

—JEFF—

I'm not a financial advisor or a debt relief consultant, and I'm certainly not going to give anyone, outside of our immediate family, advice on budgeting, saving, investing, mortgages, or car loans. I will say what we did was to work darn hard to save enough money to make sure none of our kids went into the world after college with debt. We also made a conscientious decision to enter retirement with no debt, not even a mortgage. Being debt-free is being free, and we love it. There are many Dave Ramsey Financial Peace graduates, retired or not, who will tell you they feel the same way.

The apostle Timothy doesn't say that money is the root of all evil. He says, "For the **love** of money is a root of all kinds of evil" (I Timothy 6:10). Money is the last thing many of us want to relinquish control of in our lives, and giving money back to God isn't natural at first. Buying food and clothing, paying for the mortgage, taking a vacation, and then, if there's a little left in the wallet, giving some of it to the church on Sunday seems more natural. After all, God doesn't want our money, He wants our hearts, right? That's what I had falsely believed. When I finally dropped the excuses and took that leap of faith to thank, honor, and trust God by offering the firstfruits of my labor (my income), I discovered a joy few things in life can match. When Becky and I married, we agreed to tithe our joint incomes. Then, after many years of witnessing the incredible ways God used our (and many others') weekly commitment, we decided to give above and beyond the firstfruits of our labor. That too took a leap of faith, but we never once regretted it. Whether giving through the church or directly to a charity, God blesses us and our family.

God hasn't always blessed us financially from giving. Sometimes His blessings have been the gift of a new friendship, staying Covid-free in the middle of a pandemic, feeling welcomed in a new church, and beautiful grandchildren.

The apostle James writes that the "body without the spirit is dead, so faith without deeds is dead" (James 2:26). We try to live out our faith by giving our time, our talents, or our treasures, not just hold onto them. Yet too often, and without much forethought, we can find ourselves slipping back into focusing way too much on stuff that brings only temporary happiness. Hypocritical? Maybe. Frustrating? For sure. Red Rocks Church loves to say, "We are just imperfect people pursuing a perfect God," so we remind each other of that truth, release the guilt, and get back to living our faith through giving financially and through service to others, knowing that each act brings glory to the only One who truly deserves it.

Questions for Discussion

What are your thoughts about charitable giving and volunteering your time for a good cause?

_____

_____

_____

_____

Do you feel anxious about giving your money away? If so, why?

_____

_____

_____

If you are in debt, what are some steps you can take to move toward financial peace?

_____

_____

_____

_____

CHAPTER 8

STAYING CONNECTED AND SERVING ONE ANOTHER

Fitness and Health

Jeff has always been an exercise junkie. I caught the fever when we moved to Evergreen. Somewhere on our journey, we started going to the gym together at the Evergreen Recreation Center. Even the kids, mostly Brook, joined in the fun. Jeff exercised more regularly than me back then.

After I retired, I started attending the group exercise classes at the center. I loved them and was done with the sweaty gym where the high school football players would hog the equipment, do one set, and then compare their muscles in front of the mirrored wall. Even today, I still go to group classes regularly. In Evergreen, the classes were basic and fitness focused, but in Austin I started Pilates, and now, in The Woodlands, I go to Mat Pilates, barre, yoga, and other various classes. It feels so good keeping my body in motion for a couple of hours almost every day and making new friends in the process.

Back in Evergreen, Jeff and I started taking long walks around the hills in our neighborhood about four times a week. We had a specific route we took, and we talked about work, friendships, family, and our dreams; no topic was off limits. It was on one of these walks when Jeff mentioned moving back to Texas. Then we got the bicycle bug. First, we rode our bikes on a charity ride for multiple sclerosis from Denver to Ft. Collins and back the next day. Brook talked us into it and rode miles ahead of us. It was a tough ride, and we did it together (coming in last, I think). After this punishment, we went out and bought bikes and started riding the neighborhood hills together. Those hills were really challenging for me, but it was one of the activities that kept us connected.

✛ ✛ ✛

When Becky rekindled the workout bug, she began taking a P90X class at the local rec center close to where we lived in Evergreen. My image of the class was not anything like the Tony Horton P90X videos I'd seen over the years. I pictured people our age bending down touching their toes or maybe stretching their arms straight out to the side rotating clockwise then counterclockwise while holding one-pound weights. "Now hands on the hips, bend your knees, kinda"—that sort of thing. Becky convinced me to try the class with her. I'm embarrassed to say I barely finished it, and I pride myself on staying fit. Tony H. would have been proud of Becky and the group of regulars taking that class. As for me, Tony would have shaken his head and said, "Really? Go back to touching your toes, Jeff."

Becky was off the chart confident when it came to academics, especially math. On the other side of the coin, anything remotely dangerous or adventuresome made her shrink. All that began to change as the years of sobriety built upon themselves. The big turning point was our long weekend trip to La Jolla. We stayed at a golf resort called Torrey Pines. Next to the resort was a scenic state park with a hiking path that led down to the Pacific Ocean. We decided it would be fun to hike the trail one afternoon. As we headed south along the beach toward San Diego, we came upon a cliff where people launched themselves over the edge while strapped into the harness of their delta winged hang glider. We needed to get to the top of the cliff in order to close the loop on our hike. There were two ways to reach the top of the cliff: take the stairs or take the more adventurous sandy route other brave hearts had carved out heading straight up a very steep part of the cliff.

"Let's take the stairs, Jeff."

"Forget that. Let's take the trail, Becky."

"No way."

"Yes way."

"I do not like this, Jeff, but I'll try."

"That's all I can ask; let's do it."

So, we started to climb with Becky just ahead of me. The sand was soft, making the footing anything but sure, and the more we climbed the more we slid. At extremely vertical points I'd place a hand firmly on Becky's backside to keep her leaning forward. To say she never complained or cussed me out would be less than truthful, but she kept going, and we finally achieved the summit.

I say that was the turning point because several weeks later we were at Lake Powell with some of our kids, who were in college by then, and the family of the couple who invited us to be a part of the Young Life trip a few years prior. Their whole family was into mountaineering. Their son-in-law was a professional backcountry guide, so they had all the necessary gear for rappelling down the steep canyon walls of the lake.

Before climbing the cliff in La Jolla, Becky would have watched all the rappelling from the safety of the houseboat deck. New Becky strapped on the three-point harness and rappelled down the cliffs, springing off the rocks like she was a stuntperson for a *Mission Impossible* movie.

But wait, there's more. Becky also joined us for the traditional rock jumping in the afternoons. We would climb up a thirty-foot rock and run off the edge, plunging feet first into the deep water of the lake. There were also some forty- and fifty-foot rocks available for jumping, but even *Nueva* Becky has her limits. She stuck to the thirty-footer.

Getting back into road biking after decades of just mountain biking was *pura vida*, as they like to say in Costa Rica. Becky was a trouper. Being on the open road while clipped into her pedals made Becky extremely uncomfortable, especially when there was no bike lane, just a two-foot ditch waiting for its next victim. Yet, she never stopped riding with me. If anything, it made Becky more determined to overcome her fear.

While I was at work, she would strap on her bike gear and head out alone on those tough hill climbs around the neighborhood. She would usually come back with a freshly scraped knee or bruised elbow and more paint missing on the bike frame, but that never deterred her from going at it again, time after time.

✛ ✛ ✛

I have always been very competitive by nature, and that high level of competitiveness has fueled my desire to stay fit. If I don't go to the gym, hike, or get on a tennis court regularly, I start to feel anxious, even grumpy. A jittery, snarly Jeff is not a person anyone, even Becky, needs to be around. Quite frankly, I don't even want to be around myself. Caffeine withdrawl can make me grouchy but nowhere near as ornery as missing a workout or the chance to track down a little yellow ball. Long walks with Becky help me too from becoming the old man yelling, "Get off my damn grass!"

Staying fit in my early seventies helps me stay alert and improves my balance. Now that I am starting to deal with joint arthritis from repetitive injuries, exercise also minimizes the stiffness and pain I experience. The best prescription I've found for inflammation, especially after playing tennis, is ice. I'm not an ice bath plunger yet, but I do target my joints daily with ice packs. Half our freezer is now filled with ice packs. We no longer have room for three half gallons of Blue Bell ice cream. If Blue Bell markets a tub that wraps easily around my knee, I'm their first customer.

✤ ✤ ✤

When it comes to eating healthily, we have not been so good. We are working on that as we pursue a better lifestyle overall. The problem is Jeff doesn't enjoy cooking, and he has an enormous sweet tooth. (He eats whatever he wants and however much he wants and never gains a pound. So unfair.) I enjoy cooking up to a point, but it gets boring doing it all by myself. My plan is to start using an air-fryer to cook our meats and vegetables. It's simple and quick, and the cleanup (Jeff's job) isn't too time-consuming.

✛ ✛ ✛

Reports show that ultra-processed foods accelerate damage to our cells and organs as we age. The levels of obesity and chronic illness in the United States, even in the very young, makes you wonder what's going on. It seems like we have become a nation reliant on ultra-processed foods and drugs, creating a cycle of dependency, and I was no exception for much of my adult life. How can that kind of lifestyle be beneficial?

Becky and I began adhering to the 80/20 rule. We eat healthy meals eighty percent of the week. We no longer rely on microwaved dinners five nights a week, much to the disappointment of my daughter, the gourmet chef, who took great pride in relentlessly teasing us. Instead, we select organic meats and air fry them. We steam vegetables in a glass dish, not plastic bags. We focus more on fresh fruits and nuts for snacks. Additionally, we look at the sugar and chemical content in the packaged food we do buy.

When we eat healthier, we feel better, our grocery bills are lower, our energy levels stay high during the day, and we take fewer supplements. Are we strict health nuts? No, but we are making significant progress moving away from ultra-processed and toward organic. Simply put, we are trying to be better stewards of our God-given bodies. Maybe, just maybe, our grandchildren will have a life of fewer prescriptions, fewer sugar highs, and fewer sugar blues because they see Papa and CiCi eating healthy. Values are caught not taught, as the saying goes. Does that mean we won't treat them to a chili cheeseburger at Carl's Jr.? Of course not. Hey, I'm not always screaming at kids to get off my lawn.

✠ ✠ ✠

Church

Jeff and I both have a deep love for God and Jesus. We also love the three pastors that started Red Rocks Church–Austin. We felt a big loss when we moved from Austin, but we figured we would find another church we liked in The Woodlands. We have not yet. It's hard to replicate the connection we feel with this church and pastors. We make the three-hour drive to attend Red Rocks every month or so. In between we watch one of the live services online.

One weekend we went to a party thrown by the pastors at Red Rocks' first location in Austin. It was a celebration of the church's five-year anniversary. Everyone who has been instrumental in starting the church and keeping it going was invited. We drove three hours to Austin to attend, talking all the way about how we can bring the Red Rocks–Austin's church experience to The Woodlands. We came up with some good ideas together. We were so joyful when we arrived and saw all our friends from Austin. The venue was awesome. Later, there was a sit-down Italian dinner and a presentation. Our hearts were filled with joy as we learned from the pastors how giving through the church helped many individuals and organizations in the Austin community, as well as dozens of churches and ministries abroad. We know the importance of community, so we continue to seek out a new church home where there is an undeniable feeling of the Holy Spirit's presence.

Quiet Time with God

Since our time in Monterrey, Mexico, I have made a conscientious effort to spend time with God before I start my day. Early on I just read a verse or two from the *NIV Quest Study Bible*, a Bible that my very close friend, Kirk, gave me when I started regularly attending church services. Kirk somehow sensed this rookie was going to have a thousand questions about God's Word. The Quest Bible amazingly knew exactly what those questions were going to be and was ready with the answer. I literally wore that paperback version out over the next 20 years, and I replaced it with a revised hardback version that's served me well ever since.

Once I retired, work was no longer a distraction, and a few verses became a few chapters, and then those few chapters became supplemented by countless books related to what I was reading in the Bible, and that led to journaling. My favorite journal is leather bound, another gift from a dear friend and follower of Jesus.

I've always, it seems, been a late bloomer. Slow to grow, slow to comprehend math, slow to ask a girl out, because I was slow to grow, and slow to come back home to Jesus.

Here I was giving God the first part of my day, so I thought, but what I was slow to realize was the Trinity just wanted to spend time with me. Not distracted by verses or my rambling thoughts in a journal, just quiet time with me.

I certainly couldn't have a strong, knowing relationship with my loving wife if I didn't spend quiet time with her to listen, to share thoughts, to gripe, to resolve, and to celebrate, so how was I to have a fulfilling bond with my Creator if I wasn't doing the same thing with Him?

Very quickly, I discovered God, just like Becky, is a good listener and gives me the best advice.

I still read, pray, and memorize His Word. They are all critical parts of the "full armor of God" Paul, the apostle, instructs all believers to wear every day as we go out to battle the principalities of this dark world (Ephesians 6:10–18). The difference now is that I don't slap on the belt of truth, hastily pick up the sword of the Spirit, and rush out the door. I try to remember to first talk it over with my Supreme Commander.

Long Walks

Jeff and I continue to walk now that we live in The Woodlands. On the east side of town is a lake connected to a manmade waterway that is very calming and mostly shady. This is where we walk about five miles almost every day and talk about our dreams and desires. We are not spring chickens anymore and need to take better care of ourselves to be healthy for our grandchildren. I love to see my number of steps taken at the end of the day.

✢ ✢ ✢

Becky is constantly asking me to shift sides while we are walking. If there's the slightest bit of sun on the sidewalk, Becky has dibs. We laugh about it, yet I know how much she loves the feeling of the sun, so I never mind swapping sides. A well-known podcaster once said he and his wife take walks to discuss tough issues because it is hard to be confrontational when you and your spouse are looking forward and not directly at each other. That is so amazingly true for us as well.

About two miles onto our usual walking route is a long set of stairs leading up to an incredible coffee and pastry shop named Blue Door Coffee. Becky hates me for it, but I just can't walk past those stairs. There's a force always pulling me toward a great cup of coffee and, of course, a delicious sweet snack or two. That "or two" is what Becky hates, because there is just too much temptation on those plates for her not to share in my indulgence. I make it a rule to give Becky the last bite. I'd like to believe it's a selfless act, but honestly, it's my way of removing the guilt from my compulsive actions. I swear Becky is happier when we resume our walk on the Waterway. Remember our 80/20 rule? Blue Door is unashamedly eighteen and three quarters of that twenty percent.

I truly have a sweet tooth, but I cannot stand sugar in my coffee. I seldom drink soda or sweet iced tea, and my cereal of choice is straight up Grape Nuts with a dash of milk. All for the simple reason that sugar has only one essential purpose in my world and that's to make my next pastry or dessert delicious.

Lunch and Shopping

We don't have a ton of date nights, but we do like to go out to lunch after working out or during our long walks. One of our favorite places is the Blue Door where we usually split a sandwich and a sweet item. We take our time eating while we talk about what's going on in our lives and plan the rest of the day.

Close to where we live is an outdoor shopping area called Market Street. After sharing lunch, we're known to go shopping and maybe purchase something for our home or clothes for yours truly. I am so lucky that Jeff enjoys shopping with me. We also run errands and/or go to the grocery store. We love shopping together. It's part of spending time and making decisions, which is much more enjoyable together than alone.

✠ ✠ ✠

One of Becky's love languages is gifts, so blessing her is easy. I just take her to Market Street or the mall because I know how much fun she gets from trying on new clothes, and there's a big bonus for me: it's a gift to her I don't have to wrap.

Making decisions these days comes down to which color blouse or pants I need to recommend when Becky can't make up her mind. White is always the safe answer. If there is a real hard decision, I'd say it is staying within a reasonable budget. Everything looks so darn good on her, so I am more apt to blurt out "Oh, yeah, you have to get it" than to say something more sensible like "Can we wait thirty days? I was hoping we could pay our water bill this month."

Conflict Resolution

Although there is rarely much conflict in our lives now, that wasn't the case in the first five years of our marriage. Most of which was due to my drinking. The conflicts in those early years were often associated with one of us being too preferential toward one child over the others or about the amount of money I was spending. I blamed my defensiveness on my upbringing (imagine that!). I was the youngest of three girls and often felt forgotten by my parents. I was picked on a lot by my older sisters. But over the years with a lot of counseling and life coaching I've learned to let that go. I've learned to take responsibility for my actions and not let my feelings about the past fuel the conflicts here and now. That helps make for a better resolution. When we have a conflict now, we quickly reach a compromise, or one of us will acquiesce rather than fight over it.

✣ ✣ ✣

Disagreements in those early years were hard and frustrating, mostly because there was no resolution in sight. Becky played the sad childhood card, which drew a lot of sympathy from me, at first, but eventually it just became whiny background noise. My response to every impasse was "you never," "you don't," "why can't you be," "why can't you see," or even worse, I'd just go out the door and leave it unresolved.

Once Becky was sober, counseling gave us the tools to assist us in working through tough issues in a positive way. The Bible being the greatest of all those tools, especially the verse, "In your anger do not sin: Do not let the sun go down while you are still angry, and do not give the devil a foothold" (Ephesians 4:26–27).

I have always loved Becky, even when she drank. What I didn't do in those first five years was treat her as my true partner in life and value her point of view. Alcohol can damage a relationship in so many ways, including making it hard for Becky to share, with clarity, her opinions or thoughts, so I made decisions on my own.

During the past twenty sober years, we still have occasional conflicts, but the difference now is I genuinely try to show her that I respect and value her ideas whenever she expresses them. I've learned patience, though ever so slowly, and attempt not to interrupt, or even worse, complete her thoughts in mid-sentence. Is every talk perfect? No, but because now we tend to resolve issues quickly, it makes me believe that I'm much better at communicating than I was in those early years.

Serving One Another

Serving one another is one area that Jeff has down pat. Everything I know about serving others I learned by imitating him. He always lets me out the door first, opens the car door for me, asks me if there is anything he can do for me, cleans up the dishes after dinner, makes the bed in the morning, sets up the coffee, takes out the trash, pays for lunch, helps clean the house, and generally anything I ask of him. I feel like he puts me on a pedestal. I proudly wear my crown.

What do I do to serve Jeff? Let me see. Well, I totally respect him and let him lead the way. Although we do discuss matters that are important to me, I offer to help him when he's doing a project, I tell him I love him a lot and try to thank him profusely for all he does for me and us. He does more for me than vice versa. But it's not a contest. We both feel loved and cared for.

✦ ✦ ✦

Before I married Becky, I placed a higher value on lust over trust and genuine deep love. Sure, I could do nice things for my ex-wives, but it was always predicated on getting the one thing I wanted. If I didn't get it, the resentment would build.

About five years into my second marriage, we were cooped up in a hotel room for a month, waiting for the completion of our new home in Texas. Brook and Bryce were very young. They had boundless energy and constantly needed attention from their mom while I was at work. I may have been tired at the end of the day, but she was exhausted. One evening I must not have been getting the attention I thought I deserved because I lashed out and screamed at the top of my lungs, "You love those kids more than me!" It was so loud I frightened the children, and they began to cry.

Of course, she loved those children more than me in their early childhood years. How could a mother not? It's instinctual, but I was too selfish to see it. So, instead I smothered her in that tiny hotel room with undeserved guilt.

Was that moment of selfish desire to have sex the catalyst for our eventual divorce? I don't know; it certainly didn't nurture our relationship or show that I truly honored and loved her.

My pastor was also a practicing attorney, and I had reached out to him to handle my divorce. "I can be your lawyer, or I can be your pastor, but I cannot be both," he told me. I will be forever grateful to God that he helped me choose the latter.

After we divorced, I knew that if I was to ever have a lasting marriage, I needed help. Thanks again to my wise pastor, I learned the greatest secret to a lasting marriage: Serve one another.

The apostle Peter speaks at length about serving in a marriage. I had been a Christian long enough to have read his epistles multiple times, yet that wisdom never hit home in my previous marriage. I was probably too busy misinterpreting and twisting the "wives obey your husbands" passage into something I could leverage for my own benefit. But finding ways to serve Becky and not expect her to reciprocate was easier than I thought it would be. Probably because Becky appreciated the simplest of gestures: getting coffee started in the morning, making the bed, picking up kids from after-school activities, cleaning up after dinner, stopping to get half-and-half on the way home from work, lounging on the couch and rubbing her feet at the end of the day. After-school activities are decades behind me now, but I still serve her by doing the rest of those things to this day. I want continuously to demonstrate my love for Becky in those small, consistent acts of serving.

Do I still have a strong desire for intimacy with my wife? Absolutely! The difference now is that when I'm with Becky, whether it's taking her to dinner, having a date night at a concert, going on a shopping spree, or enjoying brunch on Sunday, my focus is on her, and if it leads to something beyond that, it isn't because I demand it or think I deserve it. It's because we both desire it.

Reflections on Our Story

BECKY

Staying connected is the "work" people are referring to when they say marriage takes a lot of work. You must make a concerted effort to stay connected until it is just what you do. You can stay connected by doing things together like sharing meals together, volunteering together, and even resolving conflicts together. For us, exercise is our favorite thing, and we enjoy doing it together. We also believe staying healthy for each other is important.

We have Christ as the center of our relationship. It's how our marriage has lasted twenty-five years and will continue to last many years to come. We both pray together and alone. Ask God to help you put the other person first, before your own needs. (Just do it!) Do chores together, grocery shop together, let the other person go first, and share your faith in God.

JEFF

It should be obvious by now that I love hanging out with Becky, and as much as I love exercise and competitive sports, I now love my relaxing quiet time with Becky each night even more.

There was a long period in my life when everything was a competition, and I had to win. Even when I'd go to the gym with my daughter, I just had to do one more incline sit-up than her, one more push-up, or one more minute on the stair climber at full intensity. Even now it upsets me to lose a game of Ping-Pong to Brook. The difference today is I am willing to say, "*No mas*" after she destroys me for the sixteenth consecutive time. I'm certain my loving daughter would say that's the twentieth consecutive time.

Winning is nothing compared to real peace. Walking the Waterway with Becky, sharing coffee at Blue Door, hanging out at Tommy Bahama checking the Colorado Rockies score while Bec tries on another summer dress, watching the umpteenth episode of *Suits* while rubbing Becky's feet on the couch, or watching one of the Red Rocks–Austin pastors on Sunday mornings on YouTube, those are truly wonderful moments simply because I'm sharing them with my best friend, the love of my life.

Okay, I will admit to constantly checking the mileage split times on my Apple Watch while we walk. I no doubt live a life of contradictions.

Questions for Discussion

How do you and your significant other stay connected?

_____

_____

_____

_____

Do you enjoy just hanging out with each other? Or do you do your own thing unless there is a special event?

_____

_____

_____

_____

What are some things that you both enjoy doing together?

_____

_____

_____

_____

EPILOGUE

W ell, here we are at the end of this chapter of our lives. Are we perfect? Of course not. Are our kids perfect? No, not by a long shot. They are all still finding their way, and some are further along than others. We have had some rough spots for sure, but now it seems like life is just cruising by. God has blessed us through our experiences. All I know for sure is that I love Jeff more now than the day we were married, and that love will grow more as time goes on. He is the head of our family, the glue that keeps us joined together in love.

As I look back on our story, I still feel a lot of shame about the early years and get stuck there if I'm not careful. If I'm thinking right and ask God to help me forgive myself (again), I can shake it off quickly. Jeff's unwavering love has helped me learn to love myself and right my wrongs where I am able and let the rest go. What a blessing he has been to me in our twenty-five years together.

✚ ✚ ✚

Jeff can always be relied upon to do the right thing. Those are the words of my Nana that have driven me, encouraged me, burdened me, and mostly convicted me throughout my life. The truth is I cannot be counted on to always do the right thing.

Looking back at all the bad choices I made in high school and college, I am amazed that I somehow dodged spending time in the slammer: driving intoxicated, smoking pot in public, riding a motorcycle without a license, temporarily "borrowing" school property. Any of those activities could have led to a criminal record back when I was in the halls of higher learning, and honestly, that behavior didn't end with my receiving a four-year diploma.

My life really is full of contradictions. The good news is God's Word is *not* full of contradictions, and neither is there condemnation since I accepted Jesus Christ as my Lord and Savior. Being a Christian means I can be renewed every day, and my times of *not* doing the right thing—even the ones from yesterday—can stay in the past.

If I start reliving the guilt from my bad choices, or as Pastor Ryan would say, "living frozen in time," I'm quick to recognize that it's really Satan slithering back into my life because it is the Evil One who wants me to live only in the past. So, now I declare victory over those lies by surrendering my will to the one who wants to help fight my battles, both the physical ones and the mental ones, God.

Serving Becky demonstrates a commitment beyond just our marriage vows. It truly solidifies the incredible feeling of oneness that God speaks about throughout the Bible.

My mother, Pat, was a stickler for proper grammar. Using *me* when I should have used *I* would invariably result in a gentle correction from her. Throughout her life, Mom would say to "always put the other person first." For example, it should be "Becky and me," not "me and Becky." If I could leave you with only one piece of advice, it's to never stop serving one another, or as Pat would say, "always put the other person first."

"Use your freedom to serve one another humbly in love."

— Galatians 5:13

ABOUT THE AUTHORS

When Becky and Jeff Atkinson met and fell in love in 1999, they sought a new path for marriage after both had experienced multiple failed marriages. Because they sought God as the foundation of their marriage, they were able to overcome the tumultuous first years and challenges of alcoholism, blended family, and demanding careers.

Becky is an aspiring writer and has already published her memoir, *I Drink Therefore I Am,* about her battle with alcoholism and road to recovery. By the grace of God, she recently celebrated twenty years of sobriety.

Becky and Jeff now enjoy a full life in retirement. They spend their time playing tennis, working out, taking long walks, traveling, volunteering, and enjoying their grandkids. They reside in The Woodlands, Texas.

www.ingramcontent.com/pod-product-compliance
Lightning Source LLC
Chambersburg PA
CBHW031516120626
46545CB00005B/1905